.he E•Z Legal Guide to   W9-AZU-712

Buying/Selling Your Home

E•Z Legal Books
Deerfield Beach, Florida

Copyright 1997, E-Z Legal Forms, Inc.
Printed in the United States of America

E·Z LEGAL FORMS

384 South Military Trail Deerfield Beach, FL 33442
Tel. 954-480-8933 Fax 954-480-8906
http://www.e-zlegal.com/
All rights reserved.
Distributed by E-Z Legal Forms, Inc.
...when you need it in writing! is a registered trademark of E-Z Legal Forms, Inc.
Realtor is a registered trademark of the National Association of Realtors.

... when you need it in writing! ®

1 2 3 4 5 6 7 8 9 10   CPC   10 9 8 7 6 5 4 3 2

Library of Congress Catalog Card Number:

The E-Z Legal Guide to Buying/Selling Your Home

       p.   cm.

ISBN 1-56382-411-6: $14.95

I. Title: The E-Z Legal Guide to Buying/Selling Your Home.

Buying / Selling Your Home

Important facts

Limited warranty and disclaimer

This self-help legal product is intended to be used by the consumer for his/her own benefit. It may not be reproduced in whole or in part, resold or used for commercial purposes without written permission from the publisher. In addition to copyright violations, the unauthorized reproduction and use of this product to benefit a second party may be considered the unauthorized practice of law.

This product is designed to provide authoritative and accurate information in regard to the subject matter covered. However, the accuracy of the information is not guaranteed, as laws and regulations may change or be subject to differing interpretations. Consequently, you may be responsible for following alternative procedures, or using material or forms different from those supplied with this product. It is strongly advised that you examine the laws of your state before acting upon any of the material contained in this product.

As with any legal matter, common sense should determine whether you need the assistance of an attorney. We urge you to consult with an attorney, qualified estate planner, or tax professional, or to seek any other relevant expert advice whenever substantial sums of money are involved, you doubt the suitability of the product you have purchased, or if there is anything about the product that you do not understand including its adequacy to protect you. Even if you are completely satisfied with this product, we encourage you to have your attorney review it.

It is understood that by using this kit, you are acting as your own attorney. Neither the author, publisher, distributor nor retailer are engaged in rendering legal, accounting or other professional services. Accordingly, the publisher, author, distributor and retailer shall have neither liability nor responsibility to any party for any loss or damage caused or alleged to be caused by the use of this product.

Money-back guarantee

E-Z Legal Forms offers you a limited guarantee. If you consider this product to be defective or in any way unsuitable you may return this product to us within 30 days from date of purchase for a full refund of the list or purchase price, whichever is lower. This return must be accompanied by a dated and itemized sales receipt. In no event shall our liability—or the liability of any retailer—exceed the purchase price of the product. Use of this product constitutes acceptance of these terms.

Buying / Selling Your Home

Table of contents

Buying / Selling Your Home

How to use this E-Z Legal Guide

E-Z Legal Guides can help you achieve an important legal objective conveniently, efficiently and economically. But it is nevertheless important for you to properly use this guide if you are to avoid later difficulties.

Step-by-step instructions for using this guide:

1 Carefully read all information, warnings and disclaimers concerning the legal forms in this guide. If after thorough examination you decide that you have circumstances that are not covered by the forms in this guide, or you do not feel confident about preparing your own documents, consult an attorney.

2 Complete each blank on each legal form. Do not skip over inapplicable blanks or lines intended to be completed. If the blank is inapplicable, mark "N/A" or "None" or use a dash. This shows you have not overlooked the item.

3 Always use pen or type on legal documents—never use pencil.

4 Avoid erasures and "cross-outs" on final documents. Use photocopies of each document as worksheets, or as final copies. **All documents submitted to the court must be printed on one side only.**

5 Correspondence forms may be reproduced on your own letterhead if you prefer.

6 Whenever legal documents are to be executed by a partnership or corporation, the signatory should designate his or her title.

7 It is important to remember that on legal contracts or agreements between parties all terms and conditions must be clearly stated. Provisions may not be enforceable unless in writing. All parties to the agreement should receive a copy.

8 Instructions contained in this guide are for your benefit and protection, so follow them closely.

9 You will find a glossary of useful terms at the end of this guide. Refer to this glossary if you encounter unfamiliar terms.

10 Always keep legal documents in a safe place and in a location known to your spouse, family, personal representative or attorney.

Introduction to Buying/Selling Your Home

Buying or selling a home is often the largest single transaction you make during your lifetime. If you are buying, you will likely spend much of the rest of your life paying off your home through some type of mortgage. The last thing you need to do is pay more than you can afford, or more than a house is worth. Prequalifying for a mortgage before you look at particular homes gives you focus, and consulting an appraiser can provide an honest perspective on a home's value.

If you are selling, you may have the opportunity to realize large profits, or at least cut serious losses. Be adequately prepared to seize these opportunities by properly pricing, advertising and showing your home.

Hiring a Realtor usually will cost you an additional six percent in commission. Often Realtors know little more about a property's value than you. A Realtor's ultimate goal is to make a sale and generate commission—period. The particular house you find as a buyer, or the price you settle on as a seller, is secondary. Keep this in mind before you commit, and understand the responsibilities you would take on if you decide to "go it alone."

A home is usually much more than just a financial investment—"home is where the heart is." You and your family will likely spend endless hours sleeping, eating and entertaining there. Making the right decisions before you buy or sell can help save you money or realize profit, but it can also make the difference between years of comfort and countless sleepless nights wondering where you went wrong. As a buyer, this involves prioritizing your needs and desires, thoroughly inspecting the homes you are interested in and selecting the home that is right for you.

As anyone who has bought or sold a home will attest, timing can be critical and the process quite stressful. Many sellers are also in the process of buying another home, and if they sell their home quickly they may not be able to afford to board in a hotel or stay with relatives for months while waiting to close on a new home. Likewise, many sellers will have their homes on the market for a year or more without finding a buyer. After some time, they may be forced to settle for a much lower price, especially if the buyer senses an extreme urgency to sell. In both buying and selling, desperation is costly, but it can be avoided by being prepared.

You might find the right house at the right price at the right time, and still not be in the clear. Buying or selling a home involves an intricate web of legal issues, from mortgage applications and real estate contracts to title clearances and settlement statements. This guide contains a wealth of information to help you understand basic legal issues you may confront when buying or selling a home. It also contains basic forms you may encounter.

In this guide, you will learn to judge your needs and what you can afford, whether to use a Realtor, how to evaluate and finance a home, and how to close the sale. This knowledge will save you time and money, and keep anxiety to a minimum.

CHAPTER

When to buy or sell

When to buy or sell can be as important a decision as what to buy. Consider your own personal circumstances. Is your life in transition? Maybe you need extra space or privacy because of a recent marriage or an impending birth. Or have you decided to relocate closer to work, to a better neighborhood, or to a new town altogether?

Your motivation to move may be strictly financial. Perhaps you are an apartment dweller and have decided that paying rent is merely feeding a bottomless pit. As rents rise, so do property values. Owning puts you on the profit side of the ledger. In addition, mortgage interest is tax deductible. You may use the equity in your home as leverage for other major investments, such as buying another home, sending your children to college or retiring. Financially and physically, buying a home makes for a win-win situation.

Do you have the extra money to buy your first home or to move into a nicer one? If you have been saving for some time now and have the money for a down payment, perhaps it is time. Conversely, you may decide to sell in order to repay debt, to realize a profit, to get rid of depreciating property or to upgrade (or downgrade) your living quarters.

Seasonal Cycles

Whatever your situation, you must also factor in the seasonal home sales cycles. You can take advantage of these cycles by targeting a specific group of buyers or sellers during a particular time of year.

Taxes

January, the beginning of a new tax year, is the best time for some buyers because they will have a full 12 months of mortgage interest payment deductions to reduce their income tax liability the following spring. Example: You are an independent contractor and you anticipate a particularly lucrative fiscal year. If you earn $40,000 in the coming year, the following spring you may owe as much as 28% of your income, or $11,200, before deductions. Having mortgage interest available as a tax deduction could provide substantial savings on your tax bill.

Weather

In fall and winter, home prices tend to be lower in most parts of the country because of uncertain weather and travel conditions. This especially affects vacant homes. Showing a cold home can turn buyers off and drive down the price. As a buyer, you might profit from finding a home you like during this off-season when fewer shoppers are in the market. However, at the same time fewer sellers will likely put their homes on the market, which can benefit a seller who sells during the off-season.

In spring and summer, home prices tend to rise in most parts of the country because sellers anticipate at least six months of good weather—and more daylight hours—to shop for a home, move in and make improvements. Many families with school-age children plan their home purchase around the academic year, since buying during late spring allows them to move into their new home during the summer while school is not in session.

In warm weather regions, seasonal trends reverse; the market is more active during fall and winter and drops off during spring and summer.

Holidays

The weeks surrounding Thanksgiving and Christmas and national holidays are not good times to put your home on the market. Many people travel or entertain during these times, thus reducing the pool of potential buyers.

Buyer's or seller's market

Determining whether it is a buyer's or seller's market requires extensive research and analysis. In a buyer's market, more houses are for sale than there are buyers on the market. You can likely pick and choose among a number of homes, take your time, and negotiate your price. In a seller's market, more buyers are on the market than houses being sold. Sellers can command their price, and buyers have to act quickly to finalize a sale.

Highlight

Many families with school-age children plan their home purchase around the academic year, since buying during late spring allows them to move into their new home during the summer while school is not in session.

CHAPTER 1

Having enough time

When buying you should allow yourself at least to six months in order to secure a mortgage and close on a home. If your documentation is not properly prepared, however, the process can take as long as a year. In most circumstances, time is of the essence; the quicker and more efficiently you get things done, the better.

If you are moving out of an apartment, sometimes you can arrange a month-to-month lease. However, if you are selling one house and buying another, coordinating both transactions at once and moving from one to the other can be a nearly impossible task, not to mention an expensive one. Moving and storing furniture can be costly, and you may have to rent a hotel room, put your belongings into storage, and buy a cellular phone so you can stay in touch with your contacts.

Alternatives to buying and selling

Sometimes you are simply better off not moving. Though you will rarely hear this advice from a Realtor, you may hear it from someone who has had a bad experience moving, or from someone who has successfully stayed put. The cost of the broker's commission, moving, decorating and closing—combined with the time and stress involved—could make you reconsider. You could expose yourself to possible disaster, such as an unliveable neigbhorhood, serious problems with the home, debt, or just plain homesickness. Change is not always for the better.

If your problem is not having enough space in your current home, consider remodeling or adding on. Do you like your neighborhood enough to stay? Is ample space available, and do neighborhood codes permit additions? Will the improvements boost the value of your home when you eventually sell? If the answers are "yes," financing is available. Home improvement loans are offered by the Federal Housing Admininstration and the Federal National Mortgage Association (Fannie Mae) Homestyle Program. Improving your home will build your home equity—credit measured by the difference between your home's market value and what you owe on your mortgage. Buying another home with a mortgage may drastically lower your equity.

If you think you should sell simply to pay off your debts, you should first consider refinancing, securing a second mortgage or tapping your home equity for credit. When making the decision about whether or not to

Highlight

Improving your home will build your home equity—credit measured by the difference between your home's market value and what you owe on your mortgage.

move, consult a number of sources, including not only professionals, such as an accountant, lawyer or lender, but also friends, co-workers, neighbors and relatives.

CHAPTER

What to buy or sell

Before you begin looking at homes, first consider your options. There are many types of homes to choose from: single-family, duplex, triplex, quadplex, townhome, patio home, villa, and condominium. Exploring other possibilities may be the ticket to realizing your home ownership dream.

Single-family homes

When one talks of owning "The American Dream," most likely a single-family home comes to mind. Single-family homes offer an array of benefits, along with several drawbacks. A single-family home typically provides more space and privacy than a multiple-family dwelling. The emotional attachment grows much deeper than with any other type of dwelling; a single-family home evokes a sense of pride, security, and freedom of expression. Many owners spend entire weekends mowing the lawn, manicuring the shrubbery, painting window frames, adding new furnishings, and making their home a more personalized part of their lives.

Often buyers look for homes with expansion potential. A finished basement, porch or attic may become a valuable addition. This is of particular importance in two bedroom homes, which often have limited market appeal and often can be hard to sell. Major home improvements must be weighed as investments. If you add a pool or an expensive garage to a low value house, you may not get the money back when you resell. Be sure to check codes and restrictions on the home you are considering, especially if it is in a new development. Your freedom to make additions or alterations on the property may be severely restricted.

Owning a single-family home also comes with major responsibilities. You pay for utilities, garbage removal, pesticides and just about anything else that may need care or repair. You are also head of security for your home. This may mean buying an alarm system or using a watchdog. And just like a used automobile, a previously owned home comes with its own share of defects, from a leaky faucet to a stained carpet or much worse.

Building a new home ▬▬▬▬▬▬

If you have the money for it, perhaps the best way to meet all your needs right away is to have a new home built for you. Because appliances and utilities will be modern and efficient, you should not expect repair, renovation or redecoration costs for some time. However, because a house must "settle," sometimes it takes years to "work out the bugs," from sticking windows and doors to electrical problems. Also, make sure your new home includes a lawn and some landscaping, rather than just a barren, unsightly dirt lot.

Custom versus tract

Your choice may be between a custom-designed home or a tract house, from which you choose among a variety of options. For some, building one's own home is a dream come true. To make sure it does not turn into a nightmare, check local regulations for minimum lot size and road frontage, as well as availability of water, sewer, electric and gas service. Make sure you receive all necessary permits before entering into a binding contract.

Suburban developments often show several tract home models, with options ranging from choice of setting to amenities such as a pool or bay window. A model may not meet every one of your desired specifications or help you stand out from a cookie-cutter row of neighboring homes, but would likely cost less than designing and building a home to custom specifications. And rather than just reviewing a set of blueprints, you have the advantage of seeing the actual finished product, or at least a similar one, before you buy. Builders might be unwilling to lower the the final price, but you may be able to negotiate upgraded features at no cost.

While buying a new home helps guard you against initial repairs, you also pay the price for perfection. From the purchase of property and materials to architectural work and detailed labor, it usually adds up to much more than the cost of an existing structure. You will essentially be selecting and paying for each itemized feature brand new. Property taxes tend to be high, as areas under construction still need to pay for roads, sidewalks, lighting, civic improvements, etc.

Builder support

Make sure you select a reputable builder. You can usually get information from the Better Business Bureau or a local builder's association. Owners of other houses the builder has constructed are often better sources. You can ask them if their home required any extra work after they moved in, and how the builder responded to complaints.

Construction timetable

The timetable for construction of a new home is also an important consideration. Although pre-construction prices are usually lower, sometimes you can save thousands by buying after construction is underway, especially if the buyer has backed out or defaulted, or the builder is using the home for speculation. Hiring a builder, choosing the plans, purchasing the property and closely monitoring the progress of construction all take time. A contract may or may not include deadlines. Once the builder acquires a certificate of occupancy, you will need to inspect your home and submit a "punch list" of finishing touches the builder needs to take care of. Then it is time to close the loan and take ownership of your new home.

The old "fixer-upper"

The opposite route is to buy a "fixer-upper," usually older property priced low because it is in obvious need of repair. This type of purchase can yield a prosperous return or cause nightmarish debt. Safeguard your decision by first consulting a professional inspector to uncover potential problems. Then hire an appraiser to estimate the home's current value and its projected value after improvements.

If you have proven home improvement skills, this may be the right move for you. You may uncover a palace from an often older, larger structure after only a little work. Older homes often offer more square feet and more cubic feet to work with for remodeling purposes. Some have a distinct character or an antique mystique which owners cherish. In general, they tend to be more centrally located and, in established neighborhoods, property taxes are lower.

On the other hand, you can unexpectedly encounter a series of expensive repairs. Serious repairs often involve the foundation, plumbing, electricity, or termites. They must not be ignored. Superficial repairs such

Highlight

If you have proven home improvement skills, a "fixer-upper" may be the right move for you. On the other hand, you can unexpectedly encounter a series of expensive repairs.

as new paint or landscaping are far less expensive and can be put off until you have the time and money. Practical renovations, such as remodeling the kitchen, adding bedrooms or a family room, or installing low-maintenance siding, gain back the most resale value. Be aware that the average home-improvement loan carries a much higher interest rate than a mortgage.

Advantages of owning a multi-family home

Buying a small income property with two to four apartments is similar to financing a single-family home. These multi-family homes usually can be financed with a residential mortgage typically with as little as a five percent down payment. (Residential units larger than four apartments are generally financed as commercial properties.) In addition, the buyer, as landlord, usually must agree to live on the property and is often required by the lender to have a cash reserve to cover potential rental losses for six months.

Some advantages of owning a multi-family home are:

- You may qualify for a larger mortgage than you would for a single-family home because your potential income would be larger. Lenders use tax returns or other records from the building to substantiate income from the property. If sufficient, this income can be used to qualify your own income.

- Vacancy rate. Along with rental income, the vacancy rate is crucial to the lender. Lenders use historical vacancy rates of five percent as the normal rate. A higher vacancy rate will reduce your rental income and may require a larger down payment or higher cash reserve, generally lowering your ability to qualify for the mortgage.

- Cost of maintenance. The newer the building, the lower the cost of maintenance. When deducting building expenses from your gross income, the lender wants to see five percent or less devoted to maintenance of newer buildings. Lenders use 10 percent for older buildings. A landlord living on the property can help keep maintenance costs down.

- Management fees. Be careful about management fees. When a landlord does not live on the property, a professional company is typically paid 10 percent of the gross income to manage the building. Living on the property and self-managing the building can reduce this fee and help you qualify for the loan.

Highlight

By purchasing a multi-family home, you may qualify for a larger mortgage than you would for a single family home because your potential income would be larger.

• You may be able to live on the property for very little money or even for free. This is one of the strongest motivators for becoming a landlord. This scenario works best with four rental units. At full vacancy, three of the four should be able to cover the mortgage payment, leaving the fourth free. At less than full vacancy or with fewer units, the landlord's unit may have to contribute to the monthly payment, but it should be at a substantially reduced rate.

• Tax advantages abound with ownership of multi-family dwellings. Since local laws differ, and federal laws are constantly changing, check with your accountant to see if such a purchase is suited to your own particular situation.

• Capital appreciation is another powerful motivator. Not only is there the promise of your investment being worth more than you paid for it, you can also realize a larger net profit when you sell the building. This is determined by your rental income. Because your tenants paid for much or all of your mortgage, your actual investment is reduced, allowing you a larger profit when you sell.

• As an on-premises landlord, you have greater control over your property. A properly maintained and managed property is a greater lure to potential buyers.

Disadvantages of owning a multi-family home

Owning a multi-family home is not for everyone. Here is a list of potential drawbacks:

• Because the building is more expensive, you will probably need a larger down payment than if purchasing a single-family home.

• You may be required to prove you will be a successful landlord based on your experience managing properties.

• You are dependent on rental income. If the income falls or if you have trouble collecting rent on time, you can suffer serious financial difficulties, including foreclosure.

• Your building may decline in value, especially if income falls and you can't keep up with maintenance costs. This is always a possibility when you have tenants or live in a transitional

Highlight

With a multi-family home, you are dependent on rental income. If the income falls or if you have trouble collecting rent on time, you can suffer serious financial difficulties, including foreclosure.

neighborhood. Bad tenants who cause serious damage can also impact your monthly expenses.

- Multi-family homes generally do not appreciate as rapidly or as much as single-family homes.

- When it is time to sell the property, you must draw upon a smaller pool of potential buyers than you would for a single-family home.

- You may have to live in the same building with troublesome and problematic tenants who have direct access to you.

- You have less privacy than you do in a single-family home.

- You may have trouble maintaining a business relationship with your tenants.

- You have extensive record-keeping and paperwork. Depending on the size of the property and the degree of your involvement in everyday operations, it can amount to a full-time job or more.

Other buying options

Townhomes, condominiums and villas can be less expensive and also save you time and money on maintenance. In addition, they often provide amenities you might not get from a single-family home, such as pools, health spas, tennis courts and clubhouses.

On the other hand, be sure you can live with the rules and regulations of the community. Some ban pets, work vehicles, and even motorcycles. Others restrict your ability to rent the unit.

A condominium is an owned apartment. You also own a share of common amenities, such as a pool, laundry room, and elevator. A condominium building or development has a board of directors to manage monthly maintenance and security fees and to create and enforce rules. Owning a condo entitles you to the same tax breaks as owning a single-family home.

Highlight

Owning a condo entitles you to the same tax breaks as owning a single-family home.

CHAPTER

Using a Realtor

Once you have an idea of what type of home you are after, you need to decide whether to proceed with some type of Realtor or on your own. Realtors typically charge about six percent commission on a sale. For a $100,000 house, that is $6,000!

Many real estate representatives prove to be excellent resources for finding you a home or a buyer, judging the market, and taking care of all the complicated, time-consuming tasks involved in buying or selling a home. Others have little expertise but are punchy sales personalities out to make big bucks without exerting much effort. They take short courses for certification, lack experience and receive no formal training in home appraisal.

Are the services they provide worth that much, or is it worth it to do it yourself and save the fee? If you decide to hire a representative, make sure you are comfortable with him or her and with the agreement you have signed.

Realtors, brokers and agents

Realtors go by many different names: Realtor, Realtor Associate, broker or real estate agent. A Realtor is a member of the National Association of Realtors and may include brokers or agents. A Realtor Associate works for a Realtor. A broker is licensed by the state. An agent is usually an independent contractor working for a broker.

Choosing the right Realtor

The right Realtor is the one who helps find the right home for the buyer or the right buyer for the seller. The two most common ways to find a Realtor are:

- *Word of mouth*: Friends or relatives with values similar to your own may have had success with a particular Realtor and would enthusiastically recommend that Realtor to you. This referral can be a valuable source of information. They may also tell you whom to avoid.

- *By location*: Often Realtors specialize in particular areas, developments, types of homes, builders, or just about any other method by which homes can be classified. These brokers often advertise their specialties in newspapers and local real estate publications.

Types of Realtors

Regardless of how you select a Realtor, it is important to know the different types of Realtors and whom they work for. Do not assume any Realtor you do business with is working for you. Most Realtors work *with* buyers but work *for* sellers.

This kind of Realtor is known as a *seller's broker*. This is, for example, the broker whose name appears on the "for sale" sign in the front yard. This broker has a sole and exclusive contractual responsibility to the seller, a responsibility to get the highest possible price for the home in the shortest time. The seller's broker receives a commission for the sale from the seller. You may deliver an offer to this broker and he or she is obligated to deliver it to the seller. Once an offer is accepted by the seller, it is this broker's job to keep the buyer from changing his or her mind and, thus, to close the sale.

The *buyer's broker* works exclusively for the buyer. The buyer, not the seller, pays the commission. Since sellers usually pay commissions out of the proceeds of the sale and this fee is built into the price of the home, it is said the buyer always pays the commission. However, if you as the buyer also have to pay your buyer's broker, you have an additional expense. Nevertheless, this kind of broker is increasingly popular. Because this broker's commission comes exclusively from the buyer, it is believed he or she will follow the buyer's best interests. Check your state's laws governing *agency* for the definition and legality of a buyer's broker.

A *buyer's Realtor* is the traditional real estate broker who first works for the buyer by helping to find him or her a home. But once the home is found and an offer is made, this broker's goal is to close the deal, since he or she gets paid commission by the seller. This is the most common arrangement.

Highlight

Friends or relatives may have had success with a particular Realtor and would enthusiastically recommend that Realtor to you. They may also tell you whom to avoid.

Interviewing the Realtor

To find the right Realtor, you must begin with an interview, as you would, say, with any new employee. You should ask the following questions of any potential Realtor:

1) *How long have you been with your current firm?* If the broker has been with the firm for less than a year, ask how long he or she has been a Realtor. If this is not his or her first job as a Realtor, find out where the Realtor has worked before. If the person had unrelated realty experience, such as commercial or corporate realty, ask about his or her motives for switching to residential. Always ask if the broker has plans to relocate or change jobs during the term of your contract. Look for a broker who considers this a career, not a temporary job.

2) *Can you provide past and current references?* While most brokers will readily supply references from past clients, you should also request references from current clients. Follow up on these references to get a feeling for how the broker's current relationships are doing. Ask:

   • How long was the house on the market?

   • How close to the original price did it sell for?

   • How many times did you renew the listing with the same agent?

   • Did you accept the offer based on what you thought was a good deal, or because of outside pressures?

   • Did other brokers in the office show your home to buyers?

   • Did the broker appear at the closing?

   • Was the firm generally pleasant to do business with?

   • Would you use the same broker again?

3) *What additional services can your firm provide?* Does the firm work with specific mortgage lenders, inspectors, title companies, repairmen or insurance companies? The more resources you can draw on, the more value you receive for your time and commission payout, but do find out if the real estate firm is receiving a "kickback" for delivering these services. Even so, you must balance the value of your time against paying a higher fee.

4) *What kind of game plan can you outline?* Knowing what to expect from your broker and when to expect it helps reduce some of the mystery and anxiety associated with buying or selling a home.

- Does the broker's plan seem realistic and logical?
- Does it seem well thought out based upon years of experience or is it improvised on the spot?
- Is the broker willing to justify a particular step?
- What if it just isn't working? Does the broker have an alternative plan(s)?
- Is he or she willing to customize the plan to suit your particular needs?
- Does the plan include advertising? If so, where?
- What type of market is the broker seeking?
- Is your broker willing to schedule appointments for viewing homes?

If the broker commits to a particular game plan, make sure you feel justified in relying on it. It is important that the broker be clear about your priorities so as not to waste your time.

5) *Will you screen the homes or buyers in my price range?* You don't want a broker to waste your time with properties or buyers of marginal qualification or interest. You want a broker who will sell your home or find you one within your budget.

You will want additional answers to the following questions from any potential Realtor:

- How many exclusive listings in your area has he or she had?
- How many closings in the last six months?
- What is the average time from listing to closing?
- Does the Realtor use a Multiple Listing Service or a nationwide referral service?
- How much advertising does the firm do?
- How large is his or her staff?
- Is the staff full-time or part-time?
- Does the Realtor hold open house?
- Does the Realtor help arrange financing for buyers?

Highlight

Knowing what to expect from your broker and when to expect it helps reduce some of the mystery and anxiety associated with buying or selling a home.

As a seller, do not select a broker just because he or she suggested the highest selling price. This price may be unrealistic and simply be the "bait" before the "switch" to a lower price. You also must be wary of prices that are too low. Often the broker is just looking to make a quick sale. The more brokers you interview, the easier it will be to make an informed decision. Prices that cluster around a central figure tend to be the most realistic. Throw out the highest and lowest prices.

Ask for a market analysis for your area. This should include:

Highlight

At some point you may want to change the price of your home or alter the financing arrangements. Make sure you retain the right to amend the listing at any time.

- the price that homes comparable to yours have sold for or are currently selling for
- the length of time they have been on the market
- a description of the property
- any dates of sale

After analyzing this list, establish a price with your broker based in part on how quickly you need to sell your home.

When hiring a broker to work with you, expect to sign a written agreement. This is, in effect, an employment contract, and the agreement may be informal or complex. Be sure to read it carefully, and have anything you do not understand explained in clear language.

This agreement should outline the duties and responsibilities that you and your broker have to each other. It is a good idea to insert a clause in the contract allowing you to cancel within the first 48 hours if you are not satisfied with the broker. You will, however, be responsible for the commission on any transactions, if viewed within that 48-hour period. This period of responsibility will be spelled out in the terms of your contract.

Types of listing agreements

If you are selling a home, you will be asked to sign a listing agreement. This listing outlines the terms and conditions of the sale, including whether the broker has an exclusive right, for a specified time, to market the home. At some point you may want to change the price of your home or alter the financing arrangements. Make sure you retain the right to amend the listing at any time. There are three types of listing agreements:

1) **Exclusive right to sell.** The agent who takes the listing receives a commission regardless of who actually sells the home, even if you sell the home yourself. If another broker sells the home, the commission is divided between the brokers.

2) **Exclusive agency.** You pay no commission to the broker if you sell the home yourself. This is usually used when you find someone who is interested in purchasing your home prior to hiring a broker and is often limited to that particular party.

3) **Open listing.** You pay a commission if, and only if, the broker finds a buyer before you do. Since you are willing to work at least as hard as your broker to find a buyer, brokers often accept about half the regular commission rate on this type of sale. Remember if you have an open listing with one broker, you cannot sign an exclusive agreement with another until your open listing has expired.

If the broker presents you with a buyer who is prepared to purchase your home and who meets the terms and conditions of the listing, you are obligated to pay the broker's commission. You must do this even if you reject the deal!

Commission negotiation

To successfully negotiate a lower commission, you, as buyer or seller, must be willing to share a larger part of the burden. The broker is entitled to a reasonable commission. But what is reasonable must depend upon the amount of time and effort the broker spends finding a home or buyer. If you make your own appointments from lists the broker provides, do your own chauffeuring, write your own offer, negotiate your own mortgage, and arrange for your own inspections, you should be able to convince the broker to accept less commission because he or she is providing a lower level of service. Instead of the standard six percent, you may be able to lower it to three percent. Also beware of brokers who are paid a special bonus by the seller. It may mean the selling price is far higher than the home's actual value.

Highlight

Beware of brokers who are paid a special bonus by the seller. It may mean the selling price is far higher than the home's actual value.

CHAPTER

"Going it alone"

While most people do use a Realtor's help when buying or selling a home, many people try at least once to "go it alone." Although highly motivated by the thought of saving the Realtor's commission, they are often unsuccessful. First-time buyers must beware of the usual pitfalls such as improper planning, insufficient time and lack of patience. But you *can* do it if you are market wise and adequately prepared. Before you "go it alone," learn as much as you can about the responsibilities you will be facing.

Advantages of "going it alone"

There are many advantages to "going it alone." You:

- save the cost of paying the commission to the broker
- maintain greater control and maximum flexibility over all aspects of the transaction
- decide how and when to advertise
- decide what homes to see and when to see them
- decide how to price your home
- control when and to whom you show your home
- can remain on the premises to answer questions when buyers come to inspect it
- get immediate feedback from potential buyers and sellers
- are under no obligation to accept any offer
- do not have to keep a "lock box" on your door

Disadvantages of "going it alone" ▬▬▬

"Going it alone" can also be frustrating, time-consuming and expensive. You:

- may waste time and energy seeing unqualified buyers or viewing unwanted homes
- will not get to see homes in a market that are only shown to those buyers who sign an exclusive agreement with a broker
- will have little or no access to data about past sales, current market values and conditions, multiple listing service and broker contacts
- are responsible for deciding if your initial strategy is working and for preparing alternative plans if it isn't
- have to negotiate directly with concerned parties
- will need extreme patience in dealing directly with the public on a regular basis
- will need to pay for advertising, fact sheets and open house signs, in advance
- cannot show your home when you are not there
- put undue wear and tear on your vehicle
- must seek out and investigate qualified inspectors, repairmen, lenders, surveyors, insurance companies, appraisers, title companies and attorneys

Highlight

If you are from out of town and you are not going to use a Realtor, hire an attorney for the closing because every state has different laws governing real estate sales and the transfer of property.

It is strongly recommended that you hire an appraiser if you are from out of town or are unfamiliar with the neighborhood. If you are not going to use a Realtor, hire an attorney for the closing because every state has different laws governing real estate sales and the transfer of property.

The classified ad ▬▬▬

A key element in successfully selling your own home is placing the proper ad. If you are searching for a home to buy, you must also know how to read and interpret a real estate ad. Real estate ads generally appear in the classified section of the local newspaper. Larger newspapers often have a special weekly real estate section devoted to these ads. Also, find out if any independent realty flyers are published for your area. These have smaller circulation but are exclusively targeted to home buyers, often include small photos, and can be quite effective marketing tools.

Be sure the advertising medium you choose is appropriate for your target audience. A $30,000 home may sell in a "Bargain Shopper" weekly. A $3,000,000 home would have no business in a "Bargain Shopper," or probably even the local paper, but would be better suited for a prestigious full-color statewide or regional publication.

Each word in an ad is pivotal toward describing and selling your home. Do not rely upon the classified department to write the ad for you. Have it clearly written and tested before you call the newspaper. Show it to friends or relatives and ask if they would respond to it if they were looking for a home. The ad should promote your home's features and its value, attract interest from qualified buyers and motivate them to take a serious look.

What to include in your ad

Your ad should convey the following information:

- there is no commission because you are selling the home yourself
- the home is an outstanding buy relative to similar homes on the market
- the home is open to inspection to all interested parties
- location of the home
- asking price of the home
- phone number to call for more information
- a description of the home:
    - a) style of home (ex. ranch, split level, colonial)
    - b) number of bedrooms
    - c) number of bathrooms
    - d) special rooms, such as garage, den, workshop or family room
    - e) special features, such as fireplace, pool, barbecue pit, tennis court, Jacuzzi, tiled floors, ceiling fans, bay windows, landscaping, patio, lake, etc.

Highlight

Your classified ad should promote your home's features and its value, attract interest from qualified buyers and motivate them to take a serious look.

Sample classified ad for real estate:

```
┌─────────────────────────────────────────┐
│        SOUTH ANYCITY – BY OWNER           │
│  4 BR ranch w/pool tennis lake patio      │
│  DinRm FmlyRm LivRm 3 1/2 baths           │
│  $175,000 or best reasonable offer        │
│  Inspection daily 5-8 pm Sat.-Sun.9-6     │
│  Motivated seller (123) 456-7890          │
└─────────────────────────────────────────┘
```

Basic format for the ad:

- line 1 in the sample above tells the general location and the fact that there are no commissions involved

- lines 2 and 3 describe the home and highlight its features

- line 4 suggests a negotiable starting price (If the price is not negotiable, include the word "firm.")

- line 5 explains when the home is open for inspection

- line 6 underscores that the price is negotiable and provides the telephone number to call for more information

Depending upon the description of your home, you may add or delete an item, but always include the price.

If you have written and placed a proper ad, you should receive responses the day it appears or by the next day at the latest. If you are disappointed in the number of responses, first make sure the ad ran as you placed it, and then consider altering the ad. The problem is usually the price. Even listing an undesirable address usually will attract speculators and gamblers.

For the independent buyer, classifieds can be the gateway to information. As morbid as it may sound, some buyers bargain hunt by turning to the obituary section to find out names and addresses of the deceased. After a reasonable time, they contact relatives and respectfully inquire about the sale of the vacated property.

Open house

Sellers who do without a Realtor will likely conduct an open house. A bright, attractive yard sign should include your telephone number and a convenient time to call. If potential visitors want directions, mailing or faxing them a clear map outlining the best route helps assure they won't get lost. Also make up a facts sheet describing your house and its amenities.

Highlight

Make up a facts sheet describing your house and its amenities. Most visitors are reluctant to take notes on their own, but will likely hang onto information you provide.

Most visitors are reluctant to take notes on their own, but will likely hang onto information you provide.

Once they arrive, give them a friendly greeting and a facts sheet. Ask them to sign a ledger and to provide a telephone number. Secure all small, valuable objects. Be friendly and informative, but also unobtrusive. Some visitors want to observe and comment privately. Others may want to negotiate right away. Avoid negotiating the price orally, but be prepared to have the prospective buyer complete a county-approved buyer qualification form. Ask your local county real estate board or county Board of Realtors for these forms.

CHAPTER

Can you afford it?

Before making any phone calls or visits, you must first decide what you can afford to spend on your new home. To determine an affordable price range, you need to evaluate your net worth and determine what your down payment will be.

Net worth statement

This personal financial statement of your assets and liabilities will show you the down payment you can afford. List all assets, including cash, securities, personal property, real property, pension, retirement benefits and business equity. Under debts, list all liabilities, including bills, taxes owed, mortgages, personal debts and outstanding loans. Total both columns. Subtract total debts from total assets to get your current net worth.

For an idea of what kind of monthly mortgage payment you can afford, you can generally judge by what you currently pay for housing. Then be sure to include an estimate of all additional monthly expenses involved in owning a home, such as property taxes, utilities, lawn maintenance and general repairs. Depending on the amount of your down payment, the amount of your loan, the number of points and the interest rate you receive, your mortgage payments may be less than—or greater than—your current monthly payments.

Down payment

To determine the down payment you can make, subtract from your net worth all moving and closing costs, as well as savings necessary for your retirement, emergencies, education, repairs or improvements to the new home. The result is the money available for the down payment. If you use all the money available for the down payment, your monthly payments and interest costs will be lower, but your tax deductible mortgage interest and cash available for other purposes will also be less.

When you have found the home you want to buy, begin by making an offer to purchase. This offer is made either directly to the seller or to the Realtor representing the seller, and usually is made subject to the home passing inspection. With the offer, you will be expected to deposit earnest money. Although the law does not require the deposit to be of a specific percentage, this amount is seen by the seller as a sign of your seriousness and good faith. A large deposit might give you an edge in your negotiations with the seller. In any event, your deposit must be reasonable.

Your deposit should always be made out to an escrow agent, trustee account, fiduciary agent or some other neutral person entrusted to receive your money. If you write a check for your deposit made payable to the seller, stipulate in the contract that the deposit is not to be cashed until the contract is accepted by the seller. It is a good idea to require that the deposit be placed in an interest-bearing account at the prevailing interest rate. Any interest earned should be credited toward your outstanding balance at closing. Be sure to require the return of your deposit if the seller rejects it or lets it expire.

Can you get a mortgage?

If you will need financing for the purchase of the home, you must begin applying for a mortgage as soon as your offer has been accepted by the seller; in other words, you need to prequalify for a mortgage. A mortgage is a legal document that pledges land as collateral for the repayment of a loan. The buyer is the person giving the mortgage and is called the mortgagor. The lender is the mortgagee, or creditor.

A lender takes a look at all of your information—salary, job history, credit history, debts, payment history—and then decides whether or not to loan you money (called underwriting). Some lenders also will take into account secured, guaranteed income you expect to receive in the near future, such as a government pension that is only one year away. But no lender will consider gambling winnings or overdue loan repayments.

Prequalifying

To save time and expense, some Realtors and most lenders will prequalify an applicant for free. This process essentially tells the buyer and the lender how large a mortgage the buyer can reasonably afford. Some buyers who seek this information prior to shopping for a home find

Highlight

Some buyers who prequalify prior to shopping for a home find it easier to get final approval for a mortgage.

it easier to get final approval for a mortgage. Note: *Pre-approval* is not the same as *prequalifying*. Pre-approval can be done by telephone without supplying actual documentation. It does not have the same credibility as prequalifying and is not to be relied upon by either buyer or seller.

Your credit report

Aside from having steady income, the most important factor a lender will consider will be your credit history. Every lender you approach for a mortgage will obtain your credit report, which will play a big role in their decision. Lenders hate surprises and will be very reluctant to lend against a bad and undefended credit report.

Your credit report contains a great deal of information about you. It includes items such as your name, current and previous address, social security number, job information and salary. It also contains your credit card information, bank accounts, debts and payment history, and it also may list your assets and liabilities. Your credit report can even include information that is public record, such as lawsuits and judgments, bankruptcies, divorces, foreclosures, tax liens, wage garnishments and even criminal convictions.

Any lender you approach for a loan will scrutinize your credit report, and even small problems with your credit history could make them think twice about lending you money. Before you attempt to prequalify for a mortgage, it is imperative that you obtain a copy of your credit report, examine it carefully, and clear up as many black marks or "dings" as possible. This cannot be stressed strongly enough. Not only could there be marks you have caused, it is not uncommon for mistakes to appear on your report which you will need to defend. A good place to begin is with the *E-Z Legal Credit Repair Kit*.

Highlight

Every lender you approach for a mortgage will obtain your credit report, which will play a big role in their decision. Lenders hate surprises and will be very reluctant to lend against a bad and undefended credit report.

CHAPTER

Finding the right home

Finding the right home requires planning, patience and an eye for detail. As an investor, you look for the best value and the most profit potential. As a future resident, you look for a home that best suits your needs and desires. You and your family must thoroughly examine your values and motives for buying a home. This will help you weigh your priorities as you come up with a list of tangibles you would like to see in a home. After assessing your budget, you can narrow your focus and save time by looking only at the properties you want and are able to buy.

Location, location, location

Almost universally, the two most important factors for home buyers are price and location. Once you've determined approximately how much you can afford, you must decide on an area where you would like to live. No single factor has more impact on a home's value than location. You must answer a myriad of questions regarding the location of a home:

- *Is the neighborhood safe from crime?* Ask neighbors or local police for their feelings about safety. Seeing a neighborhood at night sometimes shines a new light as well. Unlocked bicycles and open car windows at night are generally signs of a carefree environment. Bars on business windows and screaming sirens indicate a potential crime element. Can you trust that your children and your valuables will be safe?

- *Do you like the personal feel of the neighborhood?* Does it reflect your own values and personality? Perhaps you know some friends or co-workers who live there, or have said good things about it. You can meet neighbors at P.T.A. meetings, a local church, or by asking the owner to introduce you to the next door neighbor.

- *Is the local property value holding steady?* Even if the house you are viewing seems like a good deal, an undesirable neighborhood can seriously lower the property value. If the home is more expensive than most others in the neighborhood, it may not hold its resale value. Check records on real estate prices past and present and try to detect a trend. Abandoned buildings or decrepit neighboring houses are bad signs, while home improvements are positive signs. Changes in property value can result from fluctuating crime rates or changes affecting the area, such as the building of park or a nuclear power plant. You may find out about projected changes from the planning commission.

- *How far are you willing to commute?* If you do commute, are you near the highway, subway or train station you will be using? If you and your spouse will be working permanently in different parts of town, try to find a convenient midway location. Work proximity may not be a factor. You may travel to a different worksite every day, or prefer to live close to friends or recreational or entertainment attractions.

- *What school district is most desirable?* If you have school-aged children, this may be a very important factor in your decision. A quality school zone costs all tax-payers, but also boosts property values. Are any parks, libraries or other interests nearby? Will your kids have companions in their age group to play with?

- *How busy are the roads in the neighborhood?* Heavy traffic creates not only a safety hazard for the children, but also noise and air pollution. Is parking a problem?

- *Are convenient shopping centers nearby?* Will you have to travel miles to pick up groceries, or will living near a shopping center create unwanted traffic congestion?

- *What type of atmosphere do you want to live in?* Do you prefer urban, suburban or rural environs? Do you favor a wooded area or prefer it tree-free? Would you like to live on a corner, in a cul-de-sac, or in the middle of the block? Do you object to living near railroad tracks, an airport, a hill, power lines, or commercial property such as a gas station or a factory?

These are just some of the possible questions. Others will arise according to your own priorities and circumstances.

Highlight

Changes in property value can result from fluctuating crime rates or changes affecting the area, such as the building of park or a nuclear power plant.

List your needs and desires

Defining your price range and desired location is a good start to your search. Now get more specific. Think about the values and motives you have for owning a home. Recall the things you like and don't like about the houses you have been in.

First come up with a list of your needs. These are features you cannot or will not live without. An efficient heating and cooling system, safe and dependable electrical wiring, a sturdy, leak-proof roof, and good plumbing should be first on everyone's list of needs. Then there are more personal needs. Do you need a big backyard for your Doberman or a garage to store your vintage automobile? Maybe you have four growing children who each need their own bedroom.

Desires are features that you would appreciate but that are not critical to your purchase. Perhaps you would like an eat-in kitchen, a bay window or a deck. Maybe you have a special connection to a specific style of house, such as split level, ranch or colonial. Secondary concerns likely will become less important as your home hunt progresses.

Deciding on the right home requires the ability to compromise and prioritize in order to stay within your budget and get the home that's right for you. Also keep in mind that you may move again in the future. Records across the U.S. indicate families move once every four years.

Taking a tour

When you have selected several homes you would like to see, bring a map to mark locations and a pen and notebook or tape recorder to take down your initial observations so you can review them later. Write down room measurements and draw out a basic layout so you can determine if your furniture will fit. Ask questions. Get a feel for what it would be like to live there. Does it have a logical, practical layout for your needs?

Looking at a prospective home generates a wide range of emotions. Take your emotions into account, but don't let them take over. Brokers and sellers feed off prospective buyers' reactions and use them to influence your decision and weaken your negotiating position later on. Reflect on your visit. If you are interested, arrange a second visit and compile a list of questions about the property.

If your first visit was during the day, try for a night showing, or vice versa. Different lighting can expose things that had gone unnoticed, such as cracks in the plaster. Ask the seller your questions, paying special attention to facial expressions and voice inflections. No one knows the house inside and out like the owners; they can answer your questions most accurately— not always by what they say, but by how they say it.

An owner's situation or attitude can indicate how negotiations might proceed. If you discover the seller is close to bankruptcy, in the process of a divorce or a long-distance move, he or she may be ready for a quick sale. You can also get a good deal if you overlook a seller's sloppiness that does not affect the permanent condition of the home but does scare away other sellers. By the same token, don't get drawn in by a big screen TV, an afghan rug or an exquisite art collection if it is not included in the sale.

If the home passes your inspection and you are still interested, it's time to make your first monetary investment: a professional home inspection, which usually costs between $125 and $300. Look for someone who is certified by the American Society of Home Inspectors and who has no vested interest in doing the repairs themselves.

Highlight

A professional home inspection usually costs between $125 and $300. Look for someone who is certified by the American Society of Home Inspectors and who has no vested interest in doing the repairs themselves.

Making an offer

You have found a home that suits your needs in a nice location with a price you can afford. Contingent on the house passing inspection, now is a good time to make an offer. This guide contains an Offer to Purchase Real Estate form you can use for this purpose.

Here are the basic features of an offer to purchase real estate:

- it is usually accompanied by at least a $1,000 "good faith" deposit
- it effectively takes the home off the market
- it names the broker and commission to be paid by the seller
- it is contingent upon:
    a) a satisfactory inspection
    b) being free and clear of all encumbrances
- it designates the amount:
    a) due upon signing the sales agreement
    b) of the total purchase price

- it outlines the number of days the buyer has to:

    a) obtain a mortgage as detailed

    b) inspect the home

    c) make a sales agreement

    d) close on the home

- it is a binding sales contract, also known as:

    a) an agreement to buy and sell

    b) a contract of sale

Highlight

The Fair Housing Law aims to prevent discrimination in the selling, renting and financing of housing by real estate professionals.

If major repairs are needed, you have two options: you may withdraw your offer or present a lower price, factoring in the cost to fix the problems.

Discrimination

If, as a member of a racial or ethnic minority in the market to buy or sell a home, you have been discriminated against, your rights may be protected by the Fair Housing Law (Title VIII of the Civil Rights Act of 1968, amended in 1974 and 1989). It aims to prevent discrimination in the selling, renting and financing of housing by real estate professionals. The law does not apply to private individuals who own three or fewer single-family homes as long as:

- no real estate agent is used

- the advertising does not use discriminatory language

- the owner has sold no more than one home (not including a primary residence) in a two-year span

The Fair Housing Law states that no agent or lender may:

- deny you the right to buy, rent or view a home based on your race, color, national origin, religion, sex, or disability, or because you have children under 18

- urge owners to sell by saying that minorities are moving into the neighborhood

- use discriminating factors to determine the terms or conditions of a mortgage

If you believe you are a victim of discrimination, take the following steps:

- make a record of each meeting or phone call, including the person's name and title, the place, time and date each meeting occured, and a detailed account of what happened

- keep applications, receipts, business cards and all documents relevant to your case

- demand an explanation from your agent, then go to his or her employer

If your problems continue, you can write to the national, state or local fair-housing enforcement agency. You can write to Fair Housing Division, U.S. Department of Housing and Urban Development (HUD), 451 7th St., S.W., Washington, D.C., 20410-5500, or call toll-free 800-669-9777. State and local agencies will be faster; they must begin proceedings within 30 days. If you appeal to the U.S. District Court or state or local courts, you must do so within 180 days of the incident.

Obtaining
a mortgage

Often the most difficult part of buying a new home is negotiating the mortgage. Financing a home is a complicated process that is filled with changing numbers and endless choices. There are many different kinds of mortgages and many different kinds of lenders, so be sure to look at all of your options before making any final decisions.

Designing a mortgage

In the prequalifying process, you calculated your net worth and the amount of down payment you could make. Now you need to figure out how large a monthly payment you can afford to repay your loan.

Mortgage loan ratios

To establish the range of affordable monthly mortgage payments, lenders most commonly use the ratios 25/33 or 28/36. The first number in each ratio is a percentage used with your gross monthly income; the second number is also used with gross monthly income but then factored with your long-term debts. Whichever amount is lower will be the monthly payment your lender will require from you.

For example, take the often-used ratio 25/33, a gross monthly income of $1,875, and monthly credit debts of $175. Multiply 25% by $1,875 and you get a monthly mortgage payment of $468.75. Then multiply the income ($1,875) by 33% (618.75) and subtract your monthly long-term debts and credit payments ($175) to get the figure of $443.75. The lender would then choose the lower amount, or $443.75, as your monthly mortgage payment.

The first percentage is lower, but for those who have a lot of long-term debts the option of the second percentage is an obvious advantage. These budget-estimating ratios, unfortunately, lack real-world accuracy. They do not include emergency expenses, future debts, your present tax bracket, pension and Social Security deductions or any future income you might have.

Points

A point is a fee paid to a lender for obtaining the loan. It can either be paid up front or be amortized, that is, spread out in payments over the life of the loan. One point is equal to one percent of the amount of the loan, and the number of points can vary greatly. For example, a $50,000 loan with 2.5 points will amount to a $1,250 payment *in addition* to the principal and interest. Generally, the more points you have to pay, the lower your interest rate will be, and the amount is usually tax deductible. However, when refinancing, mortgage points can be assessed again, and may not be deductible. Points are one of the strongest factors in negotiating a mortgage.

Types of lenders

There are four basic lenders who may give you money:

1) **Large banks.** Traditional lenders are mainly large banks. These have the strictest requirements and qualifying formulas but often the lowest interest rates.

2) **Credit unions and hometown banks.** These are more progressive than traditional banks. In addition to past financial history, they take into account your current financial situation, present ability to pay and your financial stability.

3) **Mortgage brokers.** Mortgage brokers are financial matchmakers between lending institutions and qualified borrowers, and they closely resemble both traditional and more progressive lenders. They represent banks, organizations and private individuals with money to lend. About half of all mortgages are handled by mortgage brokers. However, with their expertise and convenience comes a fee for finding you a loan. Legitimate loan brokers usually collect their fee *after* they obtain your loan. An advance-fee loan broker, in contrast, collects *before* the loan is found. This is illegal in some states.

4) **Government agencies**. The Federal Housing Authority (FHA) and the Veteran's Administration (VA) are the two chief lenders. The FHA and the VA are actually insurers, not lenders.

Highlight

Approximately 50 percent of all mortgages are handled by mortgage brokers. However, with their expertise and convenience comes a fee for finding you a loan.

They guarantee your loan (or part of the loan) in case you default. If you qualify, you may obtain an FHA guaranteed loan for as little as five percent down payment. Although you can obtain a VA mortgage with no downpayment, VA mortgages are only available to qualifying veterans. To find out if you qualify for an FHA or VA mortgage, contact a real estate broker, your local bank, credit union, the VA or the FHA.

State financing agencies provide low-interest home financing through mortgage revenue bonds. These are Housing and Urban Development (HUD) supervised programs that require applicants to be non-homeowners during the previous three years.

Types of mortgages

Mortgages can be as creative as the people seeking them. Here are eight basic types of mortgages:

1) **Conventional mortgages.** The most common type is called a conventional mortgage, a private mortgage with a fixed term, typically 30 years, a fixed rate of interest and fixed monthly payments. Although not insured or backed by any federal or state agency, private mortgage insurance is available whereby the lender becomes the beneficiary. There are also private agencies, such as the Federal National Mortgage Association (Fannie Mae) and the Federal Home Loan Mortgage Corporation, that set guidelines for these mortgages. These agencies will buy the mortgage from the lender but only if the loan conforms to the guidelines. Typical down payments for these loans are five to 20 percent. Because your interest rate remains the same even if interest rates decline, the only way to effectively reduce it is to refinance the mortgage. The amount of money a lender is allowed to lend and the ratio of debt to property value are generally regulated by state law.

2) **Fixed-rate loans.** An increasingly common variation, this loan's faster pay-down on principal cuts the time and amount of money in half, resulting in huge savings over the life of the loan. However, monthly payments are 15 to 25 percent higher than a 30-year fixed mortgage.

3) **Adjustable rate mortgages (ARMs), variable rate mortgages (VRMs), re-negotiable rate mortgages (RRMs) and convertible mortgages.** These allow the interest rate to float or move up and down with the bank's cost of money. The rate is generally tied to an

index and remains so for a specified period of time, typically one to five years. At that time it becomes fixed at the prevailing rate, which is usually tied to the prime rate or Treasury Bill rate. The rate can often be "locked in" or converted to a conventional mortgage at any time during the floating period.

An adjustable mortgage effectively transfers risks associated with rapid interest-rate changes from the lender to the borrower. The borrower can realize substantial savings in a low-interest rate environment, but it is crucial that the interest rate be "capped," or have a fixed upper limit beyond which it cannot rise.

4) **Balloon mortgages** have an installment payment schedule and a fixed rate, but after a period of time an amount exceeding all previous payments by at least 10 percent becomes due. (Suppose you had made 12 payments of $400 for a total of $4,800. Your balloon payment might be a lump sum payment of $4,800 plus $480, or $5,200.) There may be a number of balloon payments over the life of the mortgage.

5) **Rollover mortgages** have a fixed interest rate for a portion of the mortgage, usually three to five years. After this period the rate is adjusted to meet current market conditions for another period of three to five years. This continues until the mortgage is satisfied.

6) **Graduated payment mortgages (GPMs)** allow less money to be applied toward the principal at the beginning of the mortgage to give the mortgagor time to strengthen his or her finances. While the payments are lower initially, they must increase substantially later on. This allows a buyer to purchase a more expensive home than he or she would ordinarily qualify for. However, because initial payments are low and often are not enough to cover monthly interest, later payments must be higher than they would have been with a conventional fixed mortgage.

7) **Reverse annuity mortgages** involve using the equity in a home to purchase an annuity from which monthly interest is paid.

8) **Shared appreciation mortgages (SAMs)** allow the lender to obtain an ownership interest in the property at a certain date and according to specific conditions set forth in the mortgage document.

Highlight

With an adjustable mortgage, the borrower can realize substantial savings in a low-interest rate environment, but it is crucial that the interest rate be "capped," or have a fixed upper limit beyond which it cannot rise.

Creative home financing techniques ▬

Still looking for that elusive mortgage? Consider these alternative home financing techniques:

- **Owner financing.** Sellers can finance buyers. Not only does this provide monthly income for the seller, but the seller can foreclose on the home if you, the buyer, default on your payments.

- **Lease option buying.** One way to initiate a potential sale is through a lease option. It gives the tenant a right to become comfortable with the house before committing with a big downpayment, and gives the owner immediate monthly income. The option to buy often occurs in six months to two years, and has two payment obligations: a lump sum, typically three to five percent of the price of the house, and a monthly amount—usually $50 to $300—paid in addition to rent. These payments are non-refundable and credited to the purchase price.

- **Equity sharing.** This arrangement demands an attorney because it involves complex legal considerations. An investor buys and finances a home. You agree to occupy the home and pay the mortgage through a rental fee. You also maintain the home and agree to live in the home for a specified period of time, at the end of which you can sell the home. Once the home is sold, you reimburse the investor his initial contribution and divide the remaining profit between you. The investor knows you will take care of the home because you have an equity stake in it. You also receive part of the profits and deduct the interest portion of your mortgage payments, as well as your share of the property taxes from your income taxes.

- **Co-signers.** If your credit is less than favorable, perhaps you can convince family or friends to guarantee your loan. Be careful, however, since if you default, your co-signer becomes responsible for the loan. Many banks eagerly accept a co-signer, because they then have someone financially stable to sue in case of default.

- **Pension plan borrowing.** Your pension or profit-sharing plan can lend you money based upon your contribution to the plan. The law allows you to borrow up to one-half the vested amount (your money in the plan) or $50,000, whichever is less. A plan can lend up to $10,000, regardless of the vested amount. If the loan is to purchase a principal residence, no term limit will be imposed upon the loan. If you die or retire before the full amount of the loan is repaid, the outstanding balance will be deducted from your estate.

- **Life insurance.** You can borrow against the cash or surrender value of a wholesale life or permanent life insurance policy. Many policies allow you to borrow up to 95 percent of its value, with no time limit to repay. But remember, your coverage under a policy is reduced by the amount you borrow. Outstanding balances and interest are deducted from any distributions under the policy should you die.

- **Inheritance buy-outs.** If your inheritance is held in trust or otherwise won't be available until later, you can sell rights to your inheritance or trust to companies that can wait for the funds to be released.

- **Syndicates.** Organize a group for the purpose of investing in real estate secured by your mortgage. Investors also receive equity or profits from the home.

- **Probate properties.** These are unwanted homes inherited by people who would prefer to sell them and pocket the money. Heirs are usually busy people and can be highly motivated sellers, especially if mortgage payments must be made on time. The prospects of regular monthly income may motivate them to settle with little or no cash down.

- **Union financing.** Some unions offer first-time home loans to members who pay as little as three percent down with no loan origination fees. Parents and children of union members also may qualify.

Highlight

If your inheritance is held in trust or otherwise won't be available until later, you can sell rights to your inheritance or trust to companies that can wait for the funds to be released.

The application process

During your initial interview with a loan officer you will:

- fill out a formal application
- learn about loan origination fees, usually one percent of the loan. These have to be paid prior to approval.
- pay processing, appraisal, and credit report fees, loan discount points and—if you assume a mortgage—a loan-assumption fee
- find out if your loan application is rejected. If so, will the fee be refunded?
- discover how long the prevailing interest rate is good for and when can it be locked in
- receive a good faith estimate of closing costs within three business days of completing your loan application

- determine if you need to obtain private mortgage insurance or face other special insurance considerations

Under no circumstances should you purchase credit life insurance from your lender. This can be obtained far less expensively from an independent insurance broker. It is illegal to make purchasing this insurance a condition of acceptance on the part of the lender.

Appraisals

After you receive preliminary loan approval, you will need to have the home appraised. The lender usually selects the appraiser to evaluate the value of the home. The appraiser should be licensed, specialize in residential properties and base the appraisal upon well-established criteria.

Problems may begin when the appraised value of the home is too low to justify the selling price. While most contracts contain an escape clause due to a low appraisal, you may still want to buy that particular home. Explain to the seller that the house won't sell at such a high price, and ask him to lower it. The seller may ask you to make up the difference between the asking price and the appraisal price with your own money. Avoid this because you would be paying more than the appraised value of the home and you will have less cash available.

One criteria an appraiser uses is to examine recent sales of similar homes in the neighborhood. Most appraisers use the multiple listing service to obtain reports of sales. To raise the appraised value of your home, you may need to scour public records for private sales that are not reported in the multiple listing services.

The letter of commitment

This letter from the lender guarantees you have been approved to buy the home. When you receive this letter be sure to read it carefully. You must check for errors or misunderstandings as it will outline all of the terms and conditions of the loan. If you are satisfied, sign the letter, make copies for yourself and return it to the lender.

Highlight

Most appraisers use the multiple listing service to obtain reports of sales. To raise the appraised value of your home, you may need to scour public records for private sales that are not reported in the multiple listing services.

CHAPTER

Inspection

Once an offer has been made, an inspection is necessary before you can close on the home. The professional inspector you hire will provide a thorough expert analysis of the more technical, less obvious factors. You, however, should make your own inspection, looking at the more obvious, subjective factors. You especially need to look for things that may cause you trouble and added expense down the road.

Exterior evaluation

- **Style**: Do you like the style and does it fit in with other homes in the area?

- **Foundation**: Loose bricks or uneven or corroded mortar joints can spell trouble.

- **Siding**: Looking at the house from the corners, can you detect bulges in the siding? That probably means foundation or moisture problems.

- **Doors and windows**: Open and inspect each of them. If they stick, reasons may range from fresh paint to poor installation and swelling to a bad foundation. Spongy wood trim will need replacement. Leaky sealing, sticky weather-stripping and broken springs are common problems.

- **Roof**: Tattered shingles may forecast leakage if not fixed; sagging may require major repair. Most real estate agreements include a roof inspection clause, which makes the seller responsible for up to three percent of the purchase price for repairs to correct leaks or replace any damages. If damages exceed that amount and the buyer refuses to pay the excess, the seller has the right to cancel the contract.

- **Chimneys**: Check for solid foundation and flashing between the siding and the chimney.

- **Decks and porches**: Make sure foundations, floors, steps and roofs are solid.

- **Garage**: Are exterior buildings, such as garages, sheds and gazebos attractive and in good condition? They may provide plenty of storage space, but are they practical for your needs? Because they are often not constructed or maintained with the same care as the house, they may eventually require costly repairs for termite damage, weather damage or a shoddy foundation. Put them through the same evaluation steps as the home.

- **Landscaping**: Homeowners can take considerable pride in caring for the lawn. Did the owner manicure the perfect yard, or is it more like an unexplored jungle? Do the trees, shrubs and grass appear healthy? Do gutters and sump pumps drain excess water adequately? Paved sidewalks and driveways can be nice luxuries if they are in good shape.

Interior evaluation

- **Basement/crawl space**: Crawl space floors should be 80 percent covered with plastic to allow a minimal flow of moisture. This prevents dry rot and standing water, which causes structure problems along with mold and mildew buildup.

- **Design**: Take everyday activities into consideration to determine how practical the layout is. How many rooms will you pass through when carrying groceries to the kitchen, trash outside, or laundry from the washroom to the bedroom? Is there ample closet space, especially in the bedroom and near the bathroom? Are bathrooms conveniently located? Considering door and window placement, will your furniture fit? Do you like the overall feel of the house?

- **Floors and floor coverings**: Do they bubble, creek or sag under your feet? Sometimes carpet can be hiding a beautiful wood floor. Is the wood floor, carpet or vinyl stained or worn? Is the carpet pad springy? You shouldn't notice any seams, bubbling, curling or yellowing on vinyl tile.

Highlight

Take everyday activities into consideration to determine how practical the layout is. How many rooms will you pass through when carrying groceries to the kitchen, trash outside, or laundry from the washroom to the bedroom?

CHAPTER 8

Highlight

Obtain an insect inspection test, which is often free, to determine any infestation or damage. Most real estate agreements include a termite inspection clause.

- **Interior doors**: Do they open, close and lock easily?

- **Walls**: See if the walls bow or are covered with nail holes.

- **Ceilings**: If they appear uneven or discolored, they could require serious structural repair.

- **Lighting**: Do you prefer lamps or ceiling lights? Write down which rooms have which type of lighting.

- **Insulation**: Proper insulation can save lots of money on energy bills. Insulation is judged by its ability to stop heat loss and becomes less effective as it gets older.

- **Attic**: Could you expand your living space by finishing a room in the attic or could you use the space for storage? Check for water leaks or bowed rafters.

- **Appliances**: Does the house come with the appliances you need? Or will the ones you own fit? Test out the dishwasher, stove, garbage disposal and other appliances. Buyer's insurance often protects appliances for a year.

- **Pest control**: Obtain an insect inspection test, which is often free, to determine any infestation or damage. Most real estate agreements include a termite inspection clause. This makes the seller responsible for up to three percent of the purchase price for treatment and repair of infestation and damage by termites or any wood boring insect. If damages exceed that amount and the buyer refuses to pay the excess, the seller has the right to cancel the contract.

- **Air conditioning**: How old and in what condition is the air conditioning unit? Check to see that it operates properly.

- **Heating**: What type of heating system does the house use? Find out which rooms have vents and make sure they work. If the house's only heat source is a wood stove, you may have trouble obtaining a mortgage. It also may be a safety concern if you have young children.

- **Plumbing**: Detect any leaks. Make sure fixtures operate adequately. Check the water pressure by flushing the toilet and running the sinks at the same time. Run the shower on hot for 15 to 20 minutes to test the water heater.

- **Electricity**: Check to see that all outlets work. If the circuit breaker panel is less than 100 amp, or 200 amp if the house has electric heat or an electric stove, you could have problems.

CHAPTER

Accounting and investigating

Before you close on your home, you will need your accounting skills to determine your total cost of purchase, also known as closing costs. Use your investigative skills to make sure your ownership will be in full legal compliance.

Closing Costs

To calculate your total cost of purchase, you need to factor in taxes, utilities, insurance, legal fees, neighborhood fees, and improvements.

Taxes

High taxes can make a property unaffordable. Find out the real estate taxes, which usually are on the listing broker's property data sheet. Double check with the seller and local tax assessor. In some areas, your rate may change once the home changes ownership and your house is assessed for tax purposes. The seller may also have a lower rate because of some type of tax abatement, sometimes given to senior citizens, veterans and certain religious organization members. Or the owner may be paying a higher rate to pay an overdue utility bill or some other penalty. Also check the schedule for property tax payment. It may be due at the end of the fiscal year or before the upcoming tax year.

Utilities

Does the house use natural gas or oil? Oil tanks buried underground can be an expensive headache if codes or laws require their removal. Sometimes grandfather regulations can protect you against this burden. Obtain records of utility bills—such as water, sewer, and garbage removal—and factor them into the overall cost of the home.

Insurance

Homeowner's insurance must be purchased prior to settlement. It should be dated as of the settlement date and the lender must be named beneficiary. While you need only cover the amount of the mortgage, consider the replacement value of your home in the event it is destroyed by fire. Depending upon the geographical location, you may also be required to purchase natural disaster insurance including flood, earthquake and hurricane insurance.

Insurance packages start with HO (homeowner's)-1, which covers hazard damages including fire, wind, explosions, smoke, broken windows along with burglary, vandalism and liability. HO-2 also covers plumbing, heating and electricity. Condominiums and townhouse units can be insured by HO-6. You can lower your rates by taking on a deductible. If you have a $500 deductible, a repair less than that amount—such as a broken window or a bicycle theft—will come out of your pocket. If you use one company to cover all your insurance needs, such as home, auto and life, you will probably save on your total bill, and save time by paying for everything at once.

Highlight

Depending upon the geographical location, you may also be required to purchase natural disaster insurance including flood, earthquake and hurricane insurance.

Investigating

Even after you have had a home inspected, you still have some investigating to do. Without considering zoning, title, water tests and environmental issues, a buyer can run into costly, time-consuming nightmares.

Zoning

Before you get ideas about building on or making changes to the property, obtain a copy of all covenants and restrictions from neighborhood developers and zoning particulars on the property. You may be surprised how strict some codes are.

Neighborhood perks and fees

Certain developments charge mandatory membership fees—and even more to use perks that may attract you like the pool, tennis court or health spa.

Liens

Check the record on mortgages, liens, or judgments against the property. Request documentation certifying that no liens will be made as a result of improvements left unpaid by the present owner.

CHAPTER 9

Clear title

This refers to the fact that you have the uncontested right to use, own, possess, control and dispose of your home. You are protected. You have the right to pass the title to your property on to someone else. But how can you be sure you are getting clear title to the property?

Hire a title insurance company, sometimes called an abstract company, to do a title search of local public records at the County Recorder's Office or the Registry of Deeds. Your lender most likely will require this. While this will provide you with a reasonable indication of the condition of the title, the only way to be absolutely sure is to take out title insurance from the company. If there is any undiscovered cloud on the title, even a clerical error, you are protected for a one-time fee. It will not, however, protect you against any defect you cause in the title.

Never take title to property unless you are fully aware of its legal condition. Common problems include zoning restrictions, easements and rights of way, community standards, encroachments upon neighbor's property, unpaid taxes, liens, lawsuits, judgments, and bankruptcy. A quitclaim deed bypasses checks on any encumbrances. This type of transaction is common among family members.

Well water

If your new home uses well water, have the water quality tested. Be sure to do this before settlement day because it often requires two tests to pass. The well's drinking water should be at least 100 feet from the waste water. Find out if the seller has had problems with the septic tank, what shape it is in, and when it was last emptied.

Perk test

If you are considering purchasing land that requires the installation of a septic tank, you must have the soil tested. Often the county will perform this test, called a perk-test. Since septic tanks are not compatible with all soils and since this test is not required to sell land, you could make a serious mistake if you buy untested land. The sale of the home should be contingent upon this test.

Highlight

Never take title to property unless you are fully aware of the title's legal condition. Common problems include zoning restrictions, easements and rights of way, community standards, encroachments upon neighbor's property, unpaid taxes, liens, lawsuits, judgments, and bankruptcy.

Environmental issues

Two environmental issues that commonly call for completely honest disclosure from the owner are lead paint and radon gas.

- *Lead paint:* Federal law now requires sellers of pre-1978 built homes to tell prospective buyers about any lead-based paint used in or around the property. Many states also require disclosure of information about asbestos and vermin infestation (including termites).

- *Radon Gas:* Radon is a colorless, odorless, radioactive gas resulting from decomposing uranium in the soil. This uranium is not negligently buried but occurs naturally in both rock and soil. Radon gas has been shown to accumulate in inadequately ventilated homes built on such rock or soil. The federal Environmental Protection Agency has found unhealthy levels of radon in every state.

Many real estate contracts contain escape clauses if dangerous levels of radon are found. If dangerous levels of radon are detected and you still want to buy the home, have a radon correction clause inserted into the contract. This makes the sale of the home contingent upon correcting the problem. It is best to have your home tested by an approved professional. Check with your state Environmental Protection Agency for more information about radon testing.

Highlight

Many real estate contracts contain escape clauses if dangerous levels of radon are found. It is best to have your home tested by an approved professional.

CHAPTER

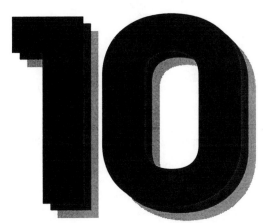

Showing your home

Perhaps the single most important factor in selling a home is its perceived value. How does your home measure up to other homes in the same price range? Does it seem to be an outstanding value? Realtors call this "showing well." A home that "shows well" commands more money and sells more quickly.

Quick-fix improvements

Since you initially get one chance to show your home to a buyer, it is the first impression that is most important. Is your home attractively packaged? If not, here's what you can do to spruce it up.

Outside

Begin with the outside of your home. What impression does it make? Instead of painting the entire exterior or replacing the siding, consider these inexpensive and easy improvements:

- repaint the front door and polish or replace the door handle

- reseal and paint the driveway

- clean and lubricate the garage door

- manicure shrubs, trees, lawn and replace plants as needed

- add new mulch and remove weeds

- repair or replace any damaged roof tiles, shingles, bricks or gutters

- resurface areas where there is cracked or peeling paint

- repair damaged or missing caulking

- wash the windows

- replace anything outside your home that is obviously **loose,** hanging, decaying or warped

Inside

Consider the interior: When potential buyers enter your **home, what** is the first thing they see? Is it a high-traffic hallway, alcove or foyer? If so, be sure this area is clean. Try brightening with fresh or artificial flowers. Pay attention to the level of lighting in your home. Many Realtors **suggest** opening all blinds, shutters and window treatments. This **allows the** maximum amount of light to enter and the home seems warmer, **brighter** and more welcoming. In addition:

- replace any cracked or broken windows

- shampoo the carpet

- repair peeling wallpaper and chipped paint

- make sure all locks work and all hinges operate smoothly

- check doorbell, chimes and alarm system

- remove mildew and stains from the bathroom

- clean and degrease the kitchen

- remove clutter and unnecessary furniture to make the **home seem** larger

- check the water pressure in faucets

- repair clogged drains

- be sure all light switches work

- service heating and cooling equipment

- wash your car if you are going to leave it in the driveway

- remove any indications of your political or religious **beliefs**

The above are simple, relatively inexpensive things that **can be done** to spruce up your home. But what about the big things? Although **there may** be things that need fixing, they do not necessarily have to be fixed **by you.** Only fix something if you can recoup the money from the buyer or if it will actually add to the perceived value of your home. The price can always be adjusted downward to reflect needed repairs, but adding the cost of repairs can easily price a home out of the market. Most experts feel the cost of major renovation does not pay if its purpose is to sell your home.

Full disclosure

In most states, if the seller of real property knows of a material defect that could not be reasonably discovered by the buyer, there is a legal obligation to disclose that defect to the buyer. If the defect is open and obvious, then the seller has no such obligation to do so. If you had no knowledge of the defect, then you have no liability. You may not hide environmental problems such as asbestos and urea formaldehyde insulation, illegal construction or alterations that violate codes, rezoning plans, neighborhood construction, or crimes which occurred in the house, any of which could affect price and desirability.

Do not deceive the buyer. Assume the buyer will ultimately discover every defect you try to hide and will do so prior to settlement day. Do not risk having the buyer renege on the deal, demand further monetary concessions for your failure to disclose, or sue you for fraudulent misrepresentation.

Highlight

Do not deceive the buyer. Assume the buyer will ultimately discover every defect you try to hide and will do so prior to settlement day.

CHAPTER

Settlement and closing

The next step after making an offer is drawing up a settlement agreement or real estate contract. The contract addresses price, property and provisions. To protect your rights and ensure you include all necessary provisions, you should hire an attorney.

The real estate contract

Most contracts contain an escape clause due to a low appraisal. However, you may still want to buy that particular home. In the contract, the buyer can revise the purchase price from the original offer. A buyer may decide to lower the offering price because of a lower-than-expected appraisal. Or he or she may sense the seller is desperate to sell and will accept less because of fear of foreclosure or lack of market interest.

Generally, large appliances such as refrigerator, stove, washer and dryer are included in the sale price of any home. Disputes often arise over chandeliers, carpeting and anything that is not nailed or bolted down. To avoid any conflict, the contract should detail exactly which appliances, furniture and extras are part of the sale.

The contract provides a closing date and may contain the phrase "time is of the essence" if needed. It also includes an escape clause, by which the seller can nullify the contract. All other agreements between the buyer and seller must be validated by the contract. No promise is binding unless included in a written contract.

Once the seller receives the contract from the buyer, he can accept it as is, reject it, or make a counter offer. A counter offer may propose altering the price, including extra items such as a satellite dish or an antique hutch, revising the closing date, or excluding certain provisions. The fewer concessions the buyer asks for beyond those of the offering agreement, the quicker negotiations will proceed. Too many changes can try the seller's patience or even cause him/her to reject the contract altogether. Agreed upon revisions must be initialed by both parties.

The owner may receive multiple offers. To make your offer stand out, you can:

- offer more than the listing price (most other bids will be below or at least match the listing price)
- offer to pay for some of the owner's expenses, such as title, appraisal or survey fees
- be flexible with closing date
- offer more earnest money
- show documented proof of mortgage prequalification
- if owner is hesitant to include an item in the sale price, offer to negotiate a price for it separately
- limit escape clauses

Pre-settlement walk-through

Prior to settlement you should inspect your new home to make sure everything that is supposed to be there is, that all repairs have been made, and that everything is in working order. Be sure to schedule your walk-through at a time of day when you have enough light to examine the grounds and outside of the home. Any last-minute changes must be reflected in your payments on settlement day.

Settlement

The settlement or closing is the final meeting between you and the seller. Attorneys representing each of you may also be present. You give the seller the down payment money and the seller gives you the home. You will have to pay the seller or his attorney by certified check. The seller or seller's attorney then pays off his mortgage and all applicable taxes. You will also pay your attorney his or her fee. Your Realtor or attorney should have given you a settlement sheet listing every fee and charge you are required to pay.

If the home is financed with an FHA-approved mortgage or is FHA-insured, you must use a HUD Settlement Statement. This approved form is

Highlight

Be sure to schedule your walk-through at a time of day when you have enough light to examine the grounds and outside of the home.

available from the title company or closing agent. Otherwise, you may use the settlement statement included in this kit.

At the settlement you may receive the following documents:

1) **Warranty deed.** Make sure it is made out exactly as you requested. It is called a warranty deed because the seller guarantees that he or she has the right to transfer title free of any defects. Some states call these deeds bargain and sale deeds, grant deeds, special warranty deeds or security deeds. The deed should be recorded in the County Recorder's Office or the Registry of Deeds.

All names must be spelled correctly. If there will be another name on your deed, one name should be followed by one of these terms:

- *tenant in common:* two or more parties own and have equal interest in the same property

- *joint tenant with right of survivorship:* same as above but survivor inherits entire property

- *tenancy by the entirety*: limited to husband and wife who own the property, as one, with survivorship, but neither spouse can sell his/her interest (not legal in every state)

These terms establish exactly what will happen to the property in the event of your death. In addition, be sure the property you are buying is accurately described with the correct legal description.

2) **Mortgage note.** This note secures the loan and outlines the specific conditions of your mortgage loan. Since it will include repayment terms, be sure you fully understand them as this note becomes legally binding once you sign it. By signing this document, you give the lender a lien on the property. If you sign a deed of trust instead of a mortgage, title is not conveyed to the lender, only the right to have the property sold in the event of default. Both the mortgage and a deed of trust should be recorded in the County Recorder's Office or the Registry of Deeds.

3) **Quitclaim deed.** If any title problems arise at the closing, these often can be handled with a quitclaim deed, whereby the person signing such a deed cedes his or her rights to the property.

4) **Affidavit.** Either buyer or seller—or both—may be asked to sign an affidavit swearing that the property is free of liens, judgments, assessments or other encumbrances.

Highlight

If any title problems arise at the closing, these often can be handled with a quitclaim deed, whereby the person signing such a deed cedes his or her rights to the property.

The buyer can expect to pay all or some of the following:

- future taxes and insurance premiums which are placed into a reserve fund or escrow account
- attorney's fees
- realtor's commission
- surveyor's fees
- recording fees, transfer taxes, appraisal, notary, and lender's attorney fees
- any costs associated with the title search

CHAPTER

Tax breaks

Buying a home is often the best investment for obtaining **tax** deductions. However, federal tax exemptions are complicated and state laws do vary depending upon the size of your estate. It may be a good idea to **hire** a tax lawyer or accountant once you have bought or sold a home. **They will** suggest you keep all records, receipts and tax returns for at least seven **years** after you have sold the house.

The three basic deductions come from mortgage interest, **property** taxes, and improvements. You can deduct all the interest you pay for **buying,** building or improving your principal residence and a second home. **Other** immediately deductible "acquisition debt," as the IRS calls it, includes **the** points paid to a lending institution for the right to borrow money. **Minor** repairs, redecorating and maintenance are not generally included **as** improvements.

The IRS also offers two special deductions on the sale of one's **main** residence: *rollover* and *one-time exclusion*.

Rollover

With the rollover plan, you must first determine the *adjusted basis* of your home. This is calculated by adding the price you paid for the home, plus improvements and minus damages, plus the gain from the sale of **a** previous home. In the eyes of the IRS, the amount of profit you make **on** selling your home is the difference between the adjusted basis and **the** amount you sell the house for. For example, a house with an adjusted basis of $65,000 that you sell for $100,000 realizes a $35,000 profit.

You may postpone paying tax on this profit as long as you replace your principal home within two years *and* the replacement home is worth at least as much as the amount realized on the sale of your previous residence. You can continue to rollover this profit indefinitly, as long as you purchase replacement homes at least equal to the amount of your sale, and purchase within the two years.

Keep in mind that the IRS is absolutely firm on the two year time period, and rollover only applies to your principal residence, not on second homes or other types of property. And, because the rollover deduction has a number of complicated provisions that would allow you to purchase a less expensive home and still meet IRS requirements, you should seek the advice of a qualified real estate professional if you are seeking this deduction.

One-time exclusion

Anyone 55 or older by the date the house is sold is entitled to a one-time tax exemption on a profit of up to $125,000. At the same 28 percent bracket, that amounts to a $35,000 tax break. Couples may use this exclusion only once.

Other deductions

You can deduct a percentage of your home expenses if you use your home for business. Calculate the percentage, in square feet or by the fraction, of the house you use for business. If you use a 20 by 20 foot room (400 square feet) and your house is 2,000 square feet, you are using 20 percent of the house. If your office takes up one level of three equally-sized floors in your home, you are using 33.3 percent. Use that percent of your yearly mortgage bill to calculate your deductible amount.

If your move is based on a job change, you can deduct some associated expenses. The IRS allows up to a $1,500 deduction for house-hunting trips and temporary living expenses but no more than $3,000 for combined moving expenses, commission, legal fees and appraisal. There is no limit for deducting your shipping and travel expenses.

Highlight

Anyone 55 or older by the date the house is sold is entitled to a one-time tax exemption on a profit of up to $125,000. Couples may use this exclusion only once.

Buying / Selling Your Home

Glossary of useful terms

A-C

Adjusted basis – The price paid for a principal residence minus the amount of any profit made from the sale of a previous home(s), according to the IRS.

Agent – A real estate representative who is usually an independent contractor working for a broker.

Amortization – To liquidate a debt by installment payments.

Appraisal – An evaluation of a home/property that determines the current value of a home by comparing it to similar homes.

Assumption of mortgage – When a third party takes over and agrees to pay the obligations of the borrower.

Balloon mortgage – A mortgage with an installment payment schedule, which also requires a lump sum payment(s) at a specific time.

Broker – A real estate representative who is licensed by the state.

Capital appreciation – The increase in market value of an asset such as a home, due to inflation or increased demand.

Clear title – Title to property for which public record shows no apparent encumbrances to the use and transfer of ownership or defects that would harm the buyer.

Closing – The procedure whereby title is transferred from seller to buyer; settlement.

Cloudy title – A dispute, lawsuit or other encumbrance which, if valid, affects the rights of the owner of the property.

Commission – A percentage of the sale price paid to a Realtor, broker or agent for services rendered.

C-M

Conveyance – The act of transferring a deed to another person.

Covenants – Clauses included in deeds or public records that prohibit or forebear specific acts.

Deed – A document used to transfer title of real property.

Deposit – Good faith, earnest money given by the buyer to the seller with an offer to purchase.

Disclosure – The legal obligation a homeowner has to inform prospective buyers of any and all defects in the home or on the property, such as environmental problems or code violations.

Equity – The amount of money the owner has invested in the property; the value of the property minus associated debts.

Encumbrance – A third party legal claim against the property.

Escrow – An arrangement whereby a third party holds funds for a buyer and seller until all terms of the agreement have been satisfied.

Floating interest rate – A variable interest rate usually tied to an index.

Foreclosure – The acquisition of real property by a lender from a mortgagor who has defaulted on the loan.

"Good faith" deposit (deposit in earnest) – An amount of money given to the seller along with an offer to purchase a home, usually subject to the home passing an inspection. The deposit is not a mortgage down payment, and the deposit is usually held by a third party until the contract is accepted by the seller.

Gross income – Total amount of income from all sources before taxes and operating expenses.

Listing – A list of properties for sale; listings can be restricted to specific housing markets, price ranges, or Realtors.

Market – A geographical area and/or specific category of potential buyers (or sellers).

Mortgage – Document pledging real property as collateral for the repayment of a loan.

M-W

Multiple listing service (MLS) – A computerized database of all properties listed for sale.

Net worth – The amount of assets you have after subtracting all of your debts and liabilities.

Open house – Making your home available for inspection (often for a day or a weekend).

Points – (also called "price points") A one-time fee charged by a lender for processing a mortgage loan. One point is equal to one percent of the amount of the loan.

Quitclaim deed – A document that transfers title and interest from seller to buyer without a warranty.

Realtor – A member of the National Association of Realtors who represents buyers/sellers of homes in the purchase/sale of real property. A Realtor may include Realtor Associates, brokers, and/or agents.

Recording – Delivering real estate documents to a public official for inclusion in the public records.

Satisfaction – A document given to the borrower by the lender indicating that the debt has been paid in full.

Settlement statement – A full and detailed accounting of the sources and dispersion of all funds in a real estate transaction.

Title – The document that describes the ownership of real property.

Title company – A company whose business is to search the public records to determine the status or condition of the title to a parcel of real property.

Underwriting – The process lenders undertake to determine whether a buyer will qualify for a mortgage loan.

Warranty deed – A document that guarantees the seller is transferring a clear title to the buyer.

Buying / Selling Your Home

Forms in this guide

NOTICE

While the forms and documents in this guide generally conform to the requirements of courts and real estate boards nationwide, certain courts and realty boards may have additional requirements or may use alternative forms and documents. Before completing and filing any forms or documents in this guide, check with the clerk of the court and the appropriate county board of realty concerning these requirements.

ADDRESS CHANGE NOTICE

Date:

To:

Dear

     Please be advised that effective   , 19   ,

our address has been changed from:

_____

_____

to

_____

_____

     Our new telephone number is:

     Please make note of the above information and direct all correspondence to us at our new

address. Thank you.

_____

AGREEMENT TO SELL REAL ESTATE

_____, of
_____ as Seller, and
_____, of
_____ as Buyer, hereby agree that the Seller shall sell and the Buyer shall buy the following described property UPON THE TERMS AND CONDITIONS HEREINAFTER SET FORTH, which shall include the STANDARDS FOR REAL ESTATE TRANSACTIONS set forth within this contract.

1. LEGAL DESCRIPTION of real estate located in _____
_____ County, State of _____:

2. PURCHASE PRICE _____ Dollars. Method of Payment:

  (a) Deposit to be held in trust by _____ $_____
  (b) Approximate principal balance of first mortgage to which conveyance shall be
       subject, if any, Mortgage holder:_____ $_____
       Interest _____% per annum: Method of payment _____
  (c) Other: _____ $_____
  (d) Cash, certified or local cashier's check on closing and delivery of deed (or such
       greater or lesser amount as may be necessary to complete payment of purchase
       price after credits, adjustments and prorations). $_____

3. PRORATIONS: Taxes, insurance, interest, rents and other expenses and revenue of said property shall be prorated as of the date of closing.

4. RESTRICTIONS, EASEMENTS, LIMITATIONS: Buyer shall take title subject to: (a) Zoning, restrictions, prohibitions and requirements imposed by governmental authority, (b) Restrictions and matters appearing on the plat or common to the subdivision, (c) Public utility easements of record, provided said easements are located on the side or rear lines of the property, (d) Taxes for year of closing, assumed mortgages, and purchase money mortgages, if any, (e) Other: _____
_____. Seller warrants that there shall be no violations of building or zoning codes at the time of closing.

5. DEFAULT BY BUYER: If Buyer fails to perform any of the covenants of this contract, all money paid pursuant to this contract by Buyer as aforesaid shall be retained by or for the account of the Seller as consideration for the execution of this contract and as agreed liquidated damages and in full settlement of any claims for damages.

6. DEFAULT BY SELLER: If the Seller fails to perform any of the covenants of this contract, the aforesaid money paid by the Buyer, at the option of the Buyer, shall be returned to the Buyer on demand; or the Buyer shall have only the right of specific performance.

7. TERMITE INSPECTION: At least 15 days before closing, Buyer, at Buyer's expense, shall have the right to obtain a written report from a licensed exterminator stating that there is no evidence of live termite or other wood-boring insect infestation on said property nor substantial damage from prior infestation on said property. If there is such evidence, Seller shall pay up to three (3%) percent of the purchase price for the treatment required to remedy such infestation, including repairing and replacing portions of said improvements which have been damaged; but if the costs for such treatment or repairs exceed three (3%) percent of the purchase price, Buyer may elect to pay such excess. If Buyer elects not to pay, Seller may pay the excess or cancel the contract.

8. ROOF INSPECTION: At least 15 days before closing, Buyer, at Buyer's expense, shall have the right to obtain a written report from a licensed roofer stating that the roof is in a watertight condition. In the event repairs are required either to correct leaks or to replace damage to facia or soffit, Seller shall pay up to three (3%) percent of the purchase price for said repairs which shall be performed by a licensed roofing contractor; but if the costs for such repairs exceed three (3%) percent of the purchase price, Buyer may elect to pay such excess. If Buyer elects not to pay, Seller may pay the excess or cancel the contract.

9. OTHER INSPECTIONS: At least 15 days before closing, Buyer or his agent may inspect all appliances, air conditioning and heating systems, electrical systems, plumbing, machinery, sprinklers and pool system included in the sale. Seller shall pay for repairs necessary to place such items in working order at the time of closing. Within 48 hours before closing, Buyer shall be entitled, upon reasonable notice to Seller, to inspect the premises to determine that said items are in working order. All items of personal property included in the sale shall be transferred by Bill of Sale with warranty of title.

10. LEASES: Seller, not less than 15 days before closing, shall furnish to Buyer copies of all written leases and estoppel letters from each tenant specifying the nature and duration of the tenant's occupancy, rental rates and advanced rent and security deposits paid by tenant. If Seller is unable to obtain such letters from tenants, Seller shall furnish the same information to Buyer within said time period in the form of a seller's affidavit, and Buyer may contact tenants thereafter to confirm such information. At closing, seller shall deliver and assign all original leases to Buyer.

11. MECHANICS LIENS: Seller shall furnish to Buyer an affidavit that there have been no improvements to the subject property for 90 days immediately preceding the date of closing, and no financing statements, claims of lien or potential lienors known to Seller. If the property has been improved within that time, Seller shall deliver releases or waivers of all mechanics liens as executed by general contractors, subcontractors, suppliers and materialmen, in addition to the seller's lien affidavit, setting forth the names of all general contractors, subcontractors, suppliers and materialmen and reciting that all bills for work to the subject property which could serve as basis for mechanics liens have been paid or will be paid at closing.

12. PLACE OF CLOSING: Closing shall be held at the office of the Seller's attorney or as otherwise agreed upon.

13. TIME IS OF THE ESSENCE: Time is of the essence of this Sale and Purchase Agreement.

14. DOCUMENTS FOR CLOSING: Seller's attorney shall prepare deed, note, mortgage, Seller's affidavit, any corrective instruments required for perfecting the title, and closing statement and submit copies of same to Buyer's attorney, and copy of closing statement to the broker, at least two days prior to scheduled closing date.

15. EXPENSES: State documentary stamps required on the instrument of conveyance and the cost of recording any corrective instruments shall be paid by the Seller. Documentary stamps to be affixed to the note secured by the purchase money mortgage, intangible tax on the mortgage, and the cost of recording the deed and purchasing money mortgage shall be paid by the Buyer.

16. INSURANCE: If insurance is to be prorated, the Seller shall on or before the closing date, furnish to Buyer all insurance policies or copies thereof.

17. RISK OF LOSS: If the improvements are damaged by fire or casualty before delivery of the deed and can be restored to substantially the same condition as now within a period of 60 days thereafter, Seller shall so restore the improvements and the closing date and date of delivery of possession hereinbefore provided shall be extended accordingly. If Seller fails to do so, the Buyer shall have the option of (1) taking the property as is, together with insurance proceeds, if any, or (2) cancelling the contract, and all deposits shall be forthwith returned to the Buyer and all parties shall be released of any and all obligations and liability.

18. MAINTENANCE: Between the date of the contract and the date of closing, the property, including lawn, shrubbery and pool, if any, shall be maintained by the Seller in the condition as it existed as of the date of the contract, ordinary wear and tear excepted.

19. CLOSING DATE: This contract shall be closed and the deed and possession shall be delivered on or before the _____ day of _____ , 19 ___ , unless extended by other provisions of this contract.

20. TYPEWRITTEN OR HANDWRITTEN PROVISIONS: Typewritten or handwritten provisions inserted in this form shall control all printed provisions in conflict therewith.

21. OTHER AGREEMENTS: No agreements or representations, unless incorporated in this contract, shall be binding upon any of the parties.

22. RADON GAS DISCLOSURE. As required by law, (Landlord) (Seller) makes the following disclosure: "Radon Gas" is a naturally occurring radioactive gas that, when it has accumulated in a building in sufficient quantities, may present health risks to persons who are exposed to it over time. Levels of radon that exceed federal and state guidelines have been found in buildings in   . Additional information regarding radon and radon testing may be obtained from your county public health unit.

23. LEAD PAINT CLAUSE. "Every purchaser of any interest in residential real property on which a residential dwelling was built prior to 1978 is notified that such property may present exposure to lead from lead-based paint that may place young children at risk of developing lead poisoning. Lead poisoning in young children may produce permanent neurological damage, including learning disabilities, reduced intelligence quotient, behavioral problems and impaired memory. Lead poisoning also poses a particular risk to pregnant women. The seller of any interest in residential real estate is required to provide the buyer with any information on lead-based paint hazards from risk assessments or inspection in the seller's possession and notify the buyer of any known lead-based paint hazards. A risk assessment or inspection for possible lead-based paint hazards is recommended prior to purchase."

24. SPECIAL CLAUSES:

COMMISSION TO BROKER: The Seller hereby recognizes _____
_____as the Broker in this transaction, and agrees to pay as commission
_____% of the gross sales price, the sum of _____
_____Dollars ($_____) or one-half of the deposit in case same is forfeited by the Buyer through failure to perform, as compensation for services rendered, provided same does not exceed the full amount of the commission.

WITNESSED BY:

_____   _____
Witness   Date   Buyer   Date

_____   _____
Witness   Date   Seller   Date

ASSIGNMENT OF MORTGAGE

BE IT KNOWN, that

party of the first part,

in consideration of the sum of
Dollars ($), and other valuable considerations, received from
or on behalf of

party of
the second part, the receipt whereof is hereby acknowledged, do hereby grant, bargain, sell, assign, transfer and set over unto the said party of the second part a certain mortgage dated the day of   , 19   made by

in favor of
and recorded in Official Records Book   , page   , public land records of
County, State of   , upon the following
described parcel of land, situate and being in said County and State, to wit:

Together with the note or obligation described in said mortgage, and the moneys due and to become due thereon, with interest from the   day of   , 19   .

TO HAVE AND TO HOLD the same unto the said party of the second part, its heirs, legal representatives, successors and assigns forever.

IN WITNESS WHEREOF, I have hereunder set my hand and seal this   day of
                    , 19   .

Signed, sealed and delivered in presence of:

_____   _____
Witness   First Party

_____   _____
Witness   Second Party

State of
County of   }

On   before me,   ,
appeared
personally known to me (or proved to me on the basis of satisfactory evidence) to be the person(s) whose name(s)
is/are subscribed to the within instrument and acknowledged to me that he/she/they executed the same in his/her/their
authorized capacity(ies), and that by his/her/their signature(s) on the instrument the person(s), or the entity upon
behalf of which the person(s) acted, executed the instrument.
WITNESS my hand and official seal.

Signature_____
          Signature of Notary   Affiant
                                                    _____Known_____Produced ID
                                          Type of ID_____
                                                                    (Seal)

_____
Signature of Preparer

_____
Print name of Preparer

_____
Address of Preparer

_____
City, State, Zip

BALLOON NOTE

FOR VALUE RECEIVED, the undersigned promise to pay to the order of

         the sum of

         Dollars ($), with annual interest of   **% on any**

unpaid balance.

     This note shall be paid in   consecutive and equal installments of $

each with a first payment one   from date hereof, and the same amount **on the same**

day of each   thereafter, provided the entire principal balance and any **accrued**

but unpaid interest shall be fully paid on or before   , 19   . **This note**

may be prepaid without penalty. All payments shall be first applied to interest and **the balance to**

principal.

     This note shall be due and payable upon demand of any holder hereof should **the under-**

signed default in any payment beyond   days of its due date. All parties to **this note**

waive presentment, demand and protest, and all notices thereto. In the event of default, **the under-**

signed agree to pay all costs of collection and reasonable attorneys' fees. The undersigned **shall**

be jointly and severally liable under this note.

     Signed this   day of   , 19   .

Signed in the presence of:

_____   _____

Witness   Maker

_____   _____

Witness   Maker

COUNTER OFFER

In response to purchase and sales agreement executed and dated _____

between _____ (Buyers)

and _____ (Sellers),

for the sale of real property known as _____

_____,

Sellers make the following counter offer:

All other terms remain the same. The above counter offer, unless accepted, shall expire at _____ o'clock _____.m. on _____. A signed and properly executed copy returned to the Sellers prior to the deadline shall constitute acceptance of this offer.

Sellers shall retain the right to accept any offer tendered prior to acceptance of this counter offer.

_____   _____
Seller   Date

_____   _____
Seller   Date

_____   _____
Buyer   Date

_____   _____
Buyer   Date

DISCHARGE OF MORTGAGE

BE IT KNOWN, that for value received, we   ,

of   holders of a certain real

estate mortgage from   to

, said mortgage dated   , 19   , and recorded in Book or Volume   , **Page**

, of the   County Registry of Deeds, acknowledge full satisfaction

and discharge of same.

Signed under seal this   day of   , 19   .

_____

_____

STATE OF   }
COUNTY OF

On   before me,   , personally **appeared**
                                              , personally **known to me (or**
proved to me on the basis of satisfactory evidence) to be the person(s) whose name(s) is/are subscribed to the within instrument and acknowledged to me that he/she/they executed the same in
his/her/their authorized capacity(ies), and that by his/her/their signature(s) on the instrument **the**
person(s), or the entity upon behalf of which the person(s) acted, executed the instrument.
WITNESS my hand and official seal.

Signature_____   Affiant   _____Known   _____Unknown
                                         ID Produced_____
                                                                  (Seal)

_____   _____
Signature of Preparer   Address of Preparer

_____   _____
Print name of Preparer   City, State, Zip

ESCROW AGREEMENT

AGREEMENT between   , (Seller)
                                                                                         ,(Buyer) and
                                                                                  (Escrow Agent).

Simultaneously with the making of this Agreement, Seller and Buyer have entered into a contract (the Contract) by which Seller will sell to Buyer the following property:

The closing will take place on   , 19   , at   .m., at the offices of
                                                        , located at
              , or at such other time and place as Seller and Buyer may jointly designate in writing. Pursuant to the Contract, Buyer must deposit $ as a down payment to be held in escrow by Escrow Agent.

The $ down payment referred to hereinabove has been paid by Buyer to Escrow Agent. Escrow Agent acknowledges receipt of $ from Buyer by check, subject to collection.

If the closing takes place under the Contract, Escrow Agent at the time of closing shall pay the amount deposited with Agent to Seller or in accordance with Seller's written instructions. Escrow Agent shall make simultaneous transfer of the said property to the Buyer.

If no closing takes place under the Contract, Escrow Agent shall continue to hold the amount deposited until receipt of written authorization for its disposition signed by both Buyer and Seller. If there is any dispute as to whom Escrow Agent is to deliver the amount deposited, Escrow Agent shall hold the sum until the parties' rights are finally determined in an appropriate action or proceeding or until a court orders Escrow Agent to deposit the down payment with it. If Escrow Agent does not receive a proper written authorization from Seller and Buyer, or if an action or proceeding to determine Seller's and Buyer's rights is not begun or diligently prosecuted, Escrow Agent is under no obligation to bring an action or proceeding in court to deposit the sum held, but may continue to hold the deposit.

Escrow Agent assumes no liability except that of a stakeholder. Escrow Agent's duties are limited to those specifically set out in this Agreement. Escrow Agent shall incur no liability to anyone except for willful misconduct or gross negligence so long as the Escrow Agent acts in good faith. Seller and Buyer release Escrow Agent from any act done or omitted in good faith in the performance of Escrow Agent's duties.

Special provisions:

Whereof the parties sign their names this   day of   , 19   .

Signed in the presence of:

_____   _____
Witness   Seller

_____   _____
Witness   Buyer

_____   _____
Witness   Escrow Agent

EXCLUSIVE RIGHT TO SELL

For and in consideration of your services to be rendered in listing for sale and in undertaking to sell or find a purchaser for the property hereinafter described, the parties understand and agree that this is an exclusive listing to sell the real estate located at:

,

together with the following improvements and fixtures:

The minimum selling price of the property shall be

dollars ($), to be payable on the following terms:

You are authorized to accept and hold a deposit in the amount of

dollars ($) as a deposit and to apply such deposit on the purchase price.

If said property is sold, traded or in any other way disposed of either by us or by anyone else within the time specified in this listing, it is agreed to and understood that you shall receive from the sale or trade of said property as your commission   percent (%) of the purchase price. Should said property be sold or traded within   days after expiration of this listing agreement to a purchaser with whom you have been negotiating for the sale or trade of the property, the said commission shall be due and payable on demand.

We agree to furnish a certificate of title showing a good and merchantable title of record, and further agree to convey by good and sufficient warranty deed or guaranteed title on payment in full.

This listing contract shall continue until midnight of   , 19   .

Date:

_____
Owner

_____
Owner

I accept this listing and agree to act promptly and diligently to procure a buyer for said property.

Date:

_____

EXERCISE OF OPTION

Date:

To:

You are hereby notified that the undersigned has elected to and does hereby exercise and accept the option dated   , 19   , executed by you as seller to the undersigned as purchaser, and agrees to all terms, conditions, and provisions of the option.

_____

LEASE WITH PURCHASE OPTION

BY THIS AGREEMENT made and entered into on   , 19   , between   ,
herein referred to as Lessor, and
herein referred to as Lessee, Lessor leases to Lessee the premises situated at
                              , in the City of   , County of
, State of   , and more particularly described as follows:
together with all appurtenances, for a term of   years, to commence on
, 19   , and to end on   , 19   , at o'clock   . m.

1. Rent. Lessee agrees to pay, without demand, to Lessor as rent for the demised premises the sum of
                         Dollars ($)   per
month in advance on the   day of each calendar month beginning   ,   19
, payable at   ,
City of   , State of   , or at such other place as Lessor may designate.

2. Security Deposit. On execution of this lease, Lessee deposits with Lessor
                    Dollars ($), receipt of which is acknowledged by Lessor, as security for
the faithful performance by Lessee of the terms hereof, to be returned to Lessee, without interest, on the full and
faithful performance by him of the provisions hereof.

3.   Quiet Enjoyment.   Lessor covenants that on paying the rent and performing the covenants
herein contained, Lessee shall peacefully and quietly have, hold, and enjoy the demised premises for the agreed term.

4. Use of Premises. The demised premises shall be used and occupied by Lessee exclusively as
                         , and neither the premises nor any part thereof shall be used at any time during
the term of this lease by Lessee for any other purpose. Lessee shall comply with all the sanitary laws, ordinances,
rules, and orders of appropriate governmental authorities affecting the cleanliness, occupancy, and preservation of
the demised premises, and the sidewalks connected thereto, during the term of this lease.

5. Condition of Premises. Lessee stipulates that he has examined the demised premises, including the grounds and
all buildings and improvements, and that they are, at the time of this lease, in good order, repair, and in a safe, clean,
and tenantable condition.

6. Assignment and Subletting. Without the prior written consent of Lessor, Lessee shall not assign this lease, or sub-
let or grant any concession or license to use the premises or any part thereof. A consent by Lessor to one assignment,
subletting, concession, or license shall not be deemed to be a consent to any subsequent assignment, subletting, concession, or license. An assignment, subletting, concession, or license without the prior written consent of Lessor, or an
assignment or subletting by operation of law, shall be void and shall, at Lessor's option, terminate this lease.

7. Alterations and Improvements. Lessee shall make no alterations to the buildings or the demised premises or
construct any building or make other improvements on the demised premises without the prior written consent of
Lessor. All alterations, changes, and improvements built, constructed, or placed on the demised premises by Lessee,
with the exception of fixtures removable without damage to the premises and movable personal property, shall,
unless otherwise provided by written agreement between Lessor and Lessee, be the property of Lessor and remain
on the demised premises at the expiration or upon sooner termination of this lease.

8. Damage to Premises. If the demised premises, or any part thereof, shall be partially damaged by fire or other casualty not due to Lessee's negligence or willful act or that of his employee, family, agent, or visitor, the premises shall be promptly repaired by Lessor and there shall be an abatement of rent corresponding with the time during which, and the extent to which, the leased premises may have been untenantable; but, if the leased premises should be damaged other than by Lessee's negligence or willful act or that of his employee, family, agent, or visitor to the extent that Lessor shall decide not to rebuild or repair, the term of this lease shall end and the rent shall be prorated up to the time of the damage.

9. Dangerous Materials. Lessee shall not keep or have on the leased premises anything of a dangerous, inflammable, or explosive character that might unreasonably increase the danger of fire on the leased premises or that might be considered hazardous or extra hazardous by any responsible insurance company.

10. Utilities. Lessee shall be responsible for arranging for and paying for all utility services required on the premises, except that   shall be provided by Lessor.

11. Maintenance and Repair. Lessee will, at his sole expense, keep and maintain the leased premises and appurtenances in good and sanitary condition and repair during the term of this lease and any renewal thereof. In particular, Lessee shall keep the fixtures on or about the leased premises in good order and repair; keep the furnace clean; keep the electric bells in order; keep the walks free from dirt and debris; and, at his sole expense, shall make all required repairs to the plumbing, range, heating apparatus, and electric and gas fixtures whenever damage thereto shall have resulted from Lessee's misuse, waste, or neglect or that of his employee, family, agent, or visitor. Major maintenance and repair of the leased premises, not due to Lessee's misuse, waste, or neglect or that of his employee, family, agent, or visitor, shall be the responsibility of Lessor or his assigns. Lessee agrees that no signs shall be placed or painting done on or about the leased premises by Lessee or at his direction without the prior written consent of Lessor.

12. Right of Inspection. Lessor and his agents shall have the right at all reasonable times during the term of this lease and any renewal thereof to enter the demised premises for the purpose of inspecting the premises and all building and improvements thereon.

13. Display of Signs. During the last   days of this lease, Lessor or his agent shall have the privilege of displaying the usual "For Sale" or "For Rent" or "Vacancy" signs on the demised premises and of showing the property to prospective purchasers or tenants.

14. Subordination of Lease. This lease and Lessee's leasehold interest hereunder are and shall be subject, subordinate, and inferior to, any liens or encumbrances now or hereafter placed on the demised premises by Lessor, all advances made under any such liens or encumbrances, the interest payable on any such liens or encumbrances, and any and all renewals or extensions of such liens or encumbrances.

15. Holdover by Lessee. Should Lessee remain in possession of the demised premises with the consent of Lessor after the natural expiration of this lease, a new month-to-month tenancy shall be created between Lessor and Lessee which shall be subject to all the terms and conditions hereof but shall be terminated on   days' written notice served by either Lessor or Lessee on the other party.

16. Surrender of Premises. At the expiration of the lease term, Lessee shall quit and surrender the premises hereby demised in as good state and condition as they were at the commencement of this lease, reasonable use and wear thereof and damages by the elements excepted.

17. Default. If any default is made in the payment of rent, or any part thereof, at the times hereinbefore specified, or if any default is made in the performance of or compliance with any other term or condition hereof, this lease, at the option of Lessor, shall terminate and be forfeited, and Lessor may re-enter the premises and remove all persons therefrom. Lessee shall be given written notice of any default or breach, and termination and forfeiture of the lease shall not result if, within   days of receipt of such notice, Lessee has corrected the default or breach or has taken action reasonably likely to effect such correction within a reasonable time. Lessee shall pay all reasonable attorneys' fees necessary to enforce lessor's rights.

18. Abandonment. If at any time during the term of this lease Lessee abandons the demised premises or any part thereof, Lessor may, at his option, enter the demised premises by any means without being liable for any prosecution therefore, and without becoming liable to Lessee for damages or for any payment of any kind whatever, and may, at his discretion, as agent for Lessee, relet the demised premises, or any part thereof, for the whole or any part of the then unexpired term, and may receive and collect all rent payable by virtue of such reletting, and, at Lessor's option, hold Lessee liable for any difference between the rent that would have been payable under this lease during the balance of the unexpired term, if this lease had continued in force, and the net rent for such period realized by Lessor by means of such reletting. If Lessor's right of re-entry is exercised following abandonment of the premises by Lessee, then Lessor may consider any personal property belonging to Lessee and left on the premises to also have been abandoned, in which case Lessor may dispose of all such personal property in any manner Lessor shall deem proper and is hereby relieved of all liability for doing so.

19. Binding Effect. The covenants and conditions herein contained shall apply to and bind the heirs, legal representatives, and assigns of the parties hereto, and all covenants are to be construed as conditions of this lease.

20. Purchase Option. It is agreed that Lessee shall have the option to purchase real estate known as:

for the purchase price of   Dollars ($) with a down
payment of   Dollars ($) payable upon exercise of
said purchase option, and with a closing date no later than   days thereafter. This purchase option
must be exercised in writing no later than   ,   19   ,
but shall not be effective should the Lessee be in default under any terms of this lease or upon any termination of this lease.

21. Radon Gas Disclosure. As required by law, (Landlord) (Seller) makes the following disclosure: "Radon Gas" is a naturally occurring radioactive gas that, when it has accumulated in a building in sufficient quantities, may present health risks to persons who are exposed to it over time. Levels of radon that exceed federal and state guidelines have been found in buildings in   . Additional information regarding radon and radon testing may be obtained from your county public health unit.

22. Lead Paint Clause. "Every purchaser of any interest in residential real property on which a residential dwelling was built prior to 1978 is notified that such property may present exposure to lead from lead-based paint that may place young children at risk of developing lead poisoning. Lead poisoning in young children may produce permanent neurological damage, including learning disabilities, reduced intelligence quotient, behavioral problems and impaired memory. Lead poisoning also poses a particular risk to pregnant women. The seller of any interest in residential real estate is required to provide the buyer with any information on lead-based paint hazards from risk assessments or inspection in the seller's possession and notify the buyer of any known lead-based paint hazards. A risk assessment or inspection for possible lead-based paint hazards is recommended prior to purchase."

23. Other Options.

IN WITNESS WHEREOF, the parties have executed this lease on the day and year first above written.

_____   _____
Lessor   Lessee

_____   _____
Signature of Preparer   Address of Preparer

_____   _____
Print name of Preparer   City, State, Zip

NOTICE: State law establishes rights and obligations for parties to rental agreements. This agreement is required to comply with the Truth in Renting Act or the applicable Landlord Tenant Statute or code of your state. If you have a question about the interpretation or legality of a provision of this agreement, you may want to seek assistance from a lawyer or other qualifed person.

Contact your local county real estate board or Association of Realtors® for additional forms that may be required to meet your specific needs.

MORTGAGE BOND

KNOW ALL BY THESE PRESENTS, that

(Obligor) does hereby acknowledge that Obligor is indebted to   ,

having an office at

County of   , State of   (Obligee), in the principal

sum of

dollars ($), which sum with interest on the unpaid balances to be computed from the

date hereof at the rate of   percent (%) per annum, Obligor does covenant to pay

to Obligee, at the office of Obligee in   ,   or

such other place as Obligee may designate in writing,   dollars ($) on

the first day of   , 19   , and thereafter in   payments of

              dollars ($) on the first day of each subsequent month, until the

principal and interest are fully paid, except that the final payment of the entire indebtedness

evidenced hereby, shall be due and payable on the first of   , 19   .

The whole or any part of the principal sum and of any other sums of money secured by
the mortgage given to secure this Bond shall, at the option of Obligee, become due and payable
if default be made in any payment under this Bond or upon the happening of any default that, by
the terms of the mortgage given to secure this Bond, shall entitle the mortgagee to declare the
principal sum, or any part thereof, to be due and payable; and all the covenants, agreements,
terms, and conditions of the mortgage are incorporated in this Bond with the same force and effect
as if set forth at length.

If more than one person joins in the execution of this Bond, the relative words herein shall be read as if written in the plural, and the words "Obligor" and "Obligee" shall include their heirs, executors, administrators, successors and assigns.

Signed this   day of   , 19   .

_____
                                                Obligor

STATE OF   }
COUNTY OF

On   before me,   , personally appeared
                                                    , personally known to me (or proved to me on the basis of satisfactory evidence) to be the person(s) whose name(s) is/are subscribed to the within instrument and acknowledged to me that he/she/they executed the same in his/her/their authorized capacity(ies), and that by his/her/their signature(s) on the instrument the person(s), or the entity upon behalf of which the person(s) acted, executed the instrument. WITNESS my hand and official seal.

Signature_____   Affiant _____Known _____Unknown
                                            ID Produced_____
                                                                            (Seal)

_____
Signature of Preparer

_____
Address of Preparer

_____
Print name of Preparer

_____
City, State, Zip

MORTGAGE DEED

This Mortgage is given by   , hereinafter called Borrower, of

to   , hereinafter called Lender, which term includes any holder of this Mortgage, to secure the payment of the PRINCIPAL SUM of $ together with interest thereon computed on the outstanding balance, all as provided in a Note having the same date as this Mortgage, and also to secure the performance of all the terms, covenants, agreements, conditions and extensions of the Note and this Mortgage.

In consideration of the loan made by Lender to Borrower and for the purpose expressed above, the Borrower does hereby grant and convey to Lender, with MORTGAGE COVENANTS, the land with the buildings situated thereon and all the improvements and fixtures now and hereafter a part thereof, being more particularly described in Exhibit A attached hereto and made a part hereof and having a street address of:

Attach Property Description

Borrower further covenants and agrees that:

1. No superior mortgage or the note secured by it will be modified without the consent of Lender hereunder.

2. Borrower will make with each periodic payment due under the Note secured by this Mortgage a payment sufficient to provide a fund from which the real estate taxes, betterment assessments and other municipal charges which can become a lien against the mortgaged premises can be paid by Lender when due. This provision shall be effective only in the event that a fund for the same purpose is not required to be established by the holder of a senior mortgage.

3. In the event that Borrower fails to carry out the covenants and agreements set forth herein, the Lender may do and pay for whatever is necessary to protect the value of and the Lender's rights in the mortgaged property and any amounts so paid shall be added to the Principal Sum due the Lender hereunder.

4. As additional security hereunder, Borrower hereby assigns to Lender, Borrower's rents of the mortgaged property, and upon default the same may be collected without the necessity of making entry upon the mortgaged premises.

5. In the event that any condition of this Mortgage or any senior mortgage shall be in default for fifteen (15) days, the entire debt shall become immediately due and payable at the option of the Lender. Lender shall be entitled to collect all costs and expenses, including reasonable attorney's fees incurred.

6. In the event that the Borrower transfers ownership (either legal or equitable) or any security interest in the mortgaged property, whether voluntarily or involuntarily, the Lender may at its option declare the entire debt due and payable.

7. This Mortgage is also security for all other direct and contingent liabilities of the Borrower to Lender which are due or become due and whether now existing or hereafter contracted.

8. Borrower shall maintain adequate insurance on the property in amounts and form of coverage acceptable to Lender and the Lender shall be a named insured as its interest may appear.

9. Borrower shall not commit waste or permit others to commit actual, permissive or constructive waste on the property.

10. Borrower further covenants and warrants to Lender that Borrower is indefeasibly seized of said land in fee simple; that the Borrower has lawful authority to mortgage said land and that said land is free and clear of all encumbrances except as may be expressly contained herein.

This Mortgage is upon the STATUTORY CONDITION and the other conditions set forth herein, for breach of which Lender shall have the STATUTORY POWER OF SALE to the extent existing under State law.

Executed under seal this   day of   , 19   .

_____   _____
Borrower   Borrower

STATE OF
COUNTY OF   }

On   before me,   , personally appeared
                                                    , personally known to me (or proved to me on the basis of satisfactory evidence) to be the person(s) whose name(s) is/are subscribed to the within instrument and acknowledged to me that he/she/they executed the same in his/her/their authorized capacity(ies), and that by his/her/their signature(s) on the instrument the person(s), or the entity upon behalf of which the person(s) acted, executed the instrument. WITNESS my hand and official seal.

Signature_____

                                          Affiant   _____Known   _____Unknown
                                          ID Produced_____
                                                                                      (Seal)

_____   _____
Signature of Preparer   Address of Preparer

_____   _____
Print name of Preparer   City, State, Zip

OFFER TO PURCHASE REAL ESTATE

BE IT KNOWN, the undersigned   of

(Buyer) offers to purchase from   of

(Owner), real estate known as   ,

City/Town of   , County of   , State of

, said property more particularly described as:

and containing   square feet of land, more or less.

> The purchase price is $
> Deposit herewith paid $
> Upon signing sales agreement $
> Balance at closing $_____
> Total purchase price $

This offer is subject to Buyer obtaining a real estate mortgage for no less than

$ payable over   years with interest not to exceed   %   at

customary terms within   days from date hereof.

The broker to this transaction is   who shall be paid a com-

mission of   by seller upon closing.

This offer is further subject to Buyer obtaining a satisfactory home inspection report and

termite/pest report within   days from date hereof.

Said property is to be sold free and clear of all encumbrances, by good and marketable

title, with full possession of said property available to Buyer.

The parties agree to execute a standard purchase and sales agreement according to the

terms of this agreement within   days.

The closing shall be on or before   , 19   , at the deed recording office.

Signed this   day of   , 19   .

In the presence of:

_____   _____
Witness   Broker

_____   _____
Witness   Buyer

                                                  _____
                                                  Owner

OPEN LISTING REALTY AGREEMENT

1.   This agreement signed on the   day of   , 19   , by and between

(Owner) and

(Real Estate Broker) who agree as follows:

2.   Listing term. Owner lists the property described in Paragraph 3, with the Real Estate Broker for a period of   days, from date hereof.

3.   Description of Property. The property listed is located at

4.   Commission. The Owner agrees to pay the Real Estate Broker a commission of   % of the sale price should the Broker find a purchaser ready, willing, and able to pay at least $ for the property or such other sum as may be accepted by Owner. Said commissions are payable upon closing.

5.   Non-Exclusive. The Owner retains the right to sell the property directly on his or her own behalf with no sales commission to broker, so long as the Broker did not find this purchaser. The Owner further has the right to list the property with other brokers. If a sale is made within   months after this agreement terminates to parties found by the Real Estate Agent during the term of this agreement, and wherein the buyer has been disclosed to the Owner, the Owner shall pay the commission specified above.

6.   Forfeit of Deposit. If a deposit of money is forfeited by a purchaser produced by Broker, one half shall be retained by the Broker, providing that this amount does not exceed the commission, and one half shall be paid to the Owner.

Witnessed:

_____   _____
Witness   Owner

_____   _____
Witness   Broker

PERSONAL FINANCIAL WORKSHEET

Name:_____ Date: _____

Assets:

Cash	$_____
Checking Account(s)	$_____
Savings Account(s)	$_____
Other Savings (CDs, etc.)	$_____
Home (market value)	$_____
Other Real Estate (market value)	$_____
Household Furnishings (market value)	$_____
Automobile(s) (blue book value)	$_____
Life Insurance (cash value)	$_____
Stocks, Bonds (current value)	$_____
Retirement Plans/Profit Sharing	$_____
Other Assets	$_____
Total Assets:	**$**_____

Debts:

Mortgages (balance due)	$_____
Installment Loans (balance due)	$_____
Other Loans (balance due)	$_____
Credit Cards (balance due)	$_____
Charge Accounts (amount owed)	$_____
Insurance Premiums Due	$_____
Taxes Owed to Date	$_____
Other Debts	$_____
Total Debts:	**$**_____
Net Worth (Total Assets minus Total Debts):	**$**_____

PROPERTY FACT WORKSHEET

Address _____

Owner name _____ Phone _____

Asking price _____

Appraisal price _____

Taxes _____

Year of completion _____

Location _____

Lot size _____

Interior space _____ sq. ft.

Style _____

Bedrooms: no., size _____

Bathrooms: no., size _____

Foundation _____

Siding _____

Roof _____

Exterior Windows & Doors _____

Garage/Shed _____

Parking Area _____

Public Utilities _____

Heating/Cooling systems _____

Fireplace _____

Insulation _____

Floor coverings _____

Wall coverings _____

Closets and storage space _____

Kitchen size, style _____

Dining room _____

Living room/Family room _____

Den/Study _____

Laundry room _____

Porch/Deck _____

Appliances _____

Expansion potential _____

Other _____

Other _____

QUITCLAIM DEED

THIS QUITCLAIM DEED, Executed this   day of   ,
19   ,

by first party, Grantor,

whose post office address is

to second party, Grantee,

whose post office address is

WITNESSETH, That the said first party, for good consideration and for the sum of
Dollars ($) paid by the said second
party, the receipt whereof is hereby acknowledged, does hereby remise, release and quitclaim
unto the said second party forever, all the right, title, interest and claim which the said first party
has in and to the following described parcel of land, and improvements and appurtenances thereto in the County of   , State of   to wit:

IN WITNESS WHEREOF, The said first party has signed and sealed these presents the day and year first above written. Signed, sealed and delivered in presence of:

_____   _____
Signature of Witness   Signature of First Party

_____   _____
Print name of Witness   Print name of First Party

_____   _____
Signature of Witness   Signature of First Party

_____   _____
Print name of Witness   Print name of First Party

State of   }
County of
On   before me,   ,
appeared
personally known to me (or proved to me on the basis of satisfactory evidence) to be the person(s) whose name(s) is/are subscribed to the within instrument and acknowledged to me that he/she/they executed the same in his/her/their authorized capacity(ies), and that by his/her/their signature(s) on the instrument the person(s), or the entity upon behalf of which the person(s) acted, executed the instrument.
WITNESS my hand and official seal.

_____   Affiant _____Known_____Produced ID
Signature of Notary   Type of ID _____
                                                              (Seal)

State of   }
County of
On   before me,   ,
appeared
personally known to me (or proved to me on the basis of satisfactory evidence) to be the person(s) whose name(s) is/are subscribed to the within instrument and acknowledged to me that he/she/they executed the same in his/her/their authorized capacity(ies), and that by his/her/their signature(s) on the instrument the person(s), or the entity upon behalf of which the person(s) acted, executed the instrument.
WITNESS my hand and official seal.

_____   Affiant _____Known_____Produced ID
Signature of Notary   Type of ID _____
                                                              (Seal)

_____   _____
Signature of Preparer   Address of Preparer

_____   _____
Print name of Preparer   City, State, Zip

REALTOR CHECKLIST

Name of Realtor: _____

_____

Company: _____

_____

Phone No./Fax: _____

_____

Time with company: _____

_____

Related experience: _____

_____

Why residential: _____

_____

Future goals: _____

_____

Contract Terms: _____

_____

Fee: _____

_____

Personality: _____

_____

References: _____

_____

Other Comments: _____

_____

RELEASE AND WAIVER OF OPTION RIGHTS

The undersigned is purchaser of an option to purchase and acquire real property dated _____, 19___, executed by _____ as seller, and recorded _____ on _____, 19___, in volume _____, on page _____, of the deed records of _____ County, State of _____ .

The option expired on _____ , 19___ .

Purchaser, the sole owner and holder of the option, acknowledges that the same was not exercised prior to the expiration date, and since that date the option has been and is now void and of no effect. Purchaser hereby waives and releases all claim, right, and interest in the option, and in the real property therein described.

IN WITNESS WHEREOF, this instrument has been executed on _____ , 19___ .

_____

STATE OF
COUNTY OF }

On _____ before me, _____ , personally appeared _____ , personally known to me (or proved to me on the basis of satisfactory evidence) to be the person(s) whose name(s) is/are sub-scribed to the within instrument and acknowledged to me that he/she/they executed the same in his/her/their authorized capacity(ies), and that by his/her/their signature(s) on the instrument the person(s), or the entity upon behalf of which the person(s) acted, executed the instrument. WITNESS my hand and official seal.

Signature_____   Affiant _____Known _____Unknown
                                            ID Produced_____
                                                                        (Seal)

_____   _____
Signature of Preparer   Address of Preparer

_____   _____
Print name of Preparer   City, State, Zip

RELEASE OF CONTRACT

We hereby mutually agree that the contract of sale executed and dated _____

between _____ (Buyers)

and _____ (Sellers)

is null and void. Buyers and Sellers shall have no rights, claims, or liabilities thereunder and each

of them specifically waives any claims or rights he may have against any of the others. We fur-

ther authorize _____(escrow agent)

to release earnest money deposited to the Buyers in the amount of _____

_____ ($).

_____   _____
Seller   Date

_____   _____
Seller   Date

_____   _____
Buyer   Date

_____   _____
Buyer   Date

RELEASE OF MORTGAGE BY A CORPORATION

_____ , a corporation incorporated under the laws of the State of _____ , having its principal office at _____ , hereby certifies that the mortgage, dated _____ , 19 ___ , executed by _____ , as mortgagor, to _____ as mortgagee, and recorded _____ , 19 ___ , in the office of the _____ of the County of _____ , State of _____ , in the Book of mortgages, page _____ , together with the debt secured by said mortgage, has been fully paid, satisfied, released, and discharged, and that the property secured thereby has been released from the lien of such mortgage.

      IN WITNESS WHEREOF, _____ has caused this release to be duly signed by its _____ authorized to sign by the resolution of its board of directors and caused its corporate seal to be affixed hereto on _____ , 19 ___ .

_____

               Title:_____

STATE OF _____ }
COUNTY OF _____ }

On _____ before me, _____ , personally appeared _____ , personally known to me (or proved to me on the basis of satisfactory evidence) to be the person(s) whose name(s) is/are subscribed to the within instrument and acknowledged to me that he/she/they executed the same in his/her/their authorized capacity(ies), and that by his/her/their signature(s) on the instrument the person(s), or the entity upon behalf of which the person(s) acted, executed the instrument.
WITNESS my hand and official seal.
Signature_____

               Affiant   _____Known   _____Unknown
               ID Produced_____
                                          (Seal)

_____   _____
Signature of Preparer   Address of Preparer

_____   _____
Print name of Preparer   City, State, Zip

RESIDENTIAL LOAN APPLICATION

MORGAGE APPLIED FOR →	☐ Conventional ☐ VA ☐ FHA ☐	Amount $	Interest	No. of Months	Monthly Payment Principal & Interest	Escrow/impounds (to be collected monthly) ☐ Taxes ☐ Hazard Ins. ☐ Mtg. Ins. ☐

Prepayment Option

S U B J E C T   P R O P E R T Y

Property Street Address		City	County	State	Zip	No. of Units

Legal Description (Attach description if necessary)	Year Built

Purpose of Loan: ☐ Purchase ☐ Construction-Permanent ☐ Construction-Refinance ☐ Other (Explain)

Complete this line if Construction-Permanent or Construction-Loan →	Lot Value Data	Original Cost	Present Value (a)	Cost of Imp. (b)	Total (a + b)	Enter Total as purchase price in details ← of purchase
	Year Acquired	$	$	$	$	

Complete this line if a Refinance Loan		Purpose of Refinance	Describe Improvements ( ) made ( ) to be made
Year Acquired	Original Cost	Amt. Existing Liens	
	$	$	Cost: $

Name(s) Title Will Be Held In	Manner In Which Title Will Be Held

Source of Down Payment and Settlement Charges

This application is designed to be completed by the borrower(s) with the lender's assistance. The Co-Borrower Section and all other Co-Borrower questions must be completed and the appropriate boxes checked if ☐ another person will be jointly obligated with the Borrower on the loan, or ☐ the Borrower is relying on income from alimony, child support or separate maintenance or on the income or assets of another person as a basis for repayment of the loan, or ☐ the Borrower is married and resides, or the property is located, in a community property state.

BORROWER

Name	Age	School Yrs.

Present Address   No. Years_____   ☐ Own ☐ Rent

Street _____

City/State/Zip_____

Former Address if less than 2 years at present address

Street _____

City/State/Zip_____

Years at former address _____ ☐ Own ☐ Rent

Marital ☐ Married ☐ Separated
Status ☐ Unmarried (incl. single, divorced, widowed)

Dependents other than listed by co-borrower	No. Ages:

Name and Address of Employer	Years employed in this line of work or profession:_____ Years on the job:_____ ☐ Self Employed*

Position/Title	Type of Business

Social Security Number***	Home Phone	Business Phone

CO-BORROWER

Name	Age	School Yrs.

Present Address   No. Years_____   ☐ Own ☐ Rent

Street _____

City/State/Zip_____

Former Address if less than 2 years at present address

Street _____

City/State/Zip_____

Years at former address _____ ☐ Own ☐ Rent

Marital ☐ Married ☐ Separated
Status ☐ Unmarried (incl. single, divorced, widowed)

Dependents other than listed by co-borrower	No. Ages:

Name and Address of Employer	Years employed in this line of work or profession:_____ Years on the job:_____ ☐ Self Employed*

Position/Title	Type of Business

Social Security Number***	Home Phone	Business Phone

GROSS MONTHLY INCOME

Item	Borrower	Co-Borrower	Total
Base Empl. Income	$	$	$
Overtime			
Bonuses			
Commissions			
Dividends/Interests			
Net Rental Income			
Other ✦ (Before completing, see notice under Describe Other Income below)			
Total	$	$	$

MONTHLY HOUSING EXPENSE**

Item	Present	Proposed
Rent	$	$
First Mortgage (P & I)		
Other Financing (P & I)		
Hazard Insurance		
Real Estate Taxes		
Mortgage Insurance		
Homeowner Ass. Dues		
Other:		
Total Monthly Pmt.		
Utilities		
Total	$	$

DETAILS OF PURCHASE

Do Not Complete If Refinance

a. Purchase Price	$
b. Total Closing Costs (Est.)	
c. Prepaid Escrows (Est.)	
d. Total (a + b + c)	$
e. Amount This Mortgage	
f. Other Financing	
g. Other Equity	
h. Amount of Cash Deposit	
i. Closing Costs Paid by Seller	
j. Cash Req. for Closing (Est.)	

DESCRIBE OTHER INCOME

↓ B = Borrower   C = Co-Borrower   NOTICE: ✦ Alimony, child support, or separate maintenance income need not be revealed if the Borrower or Co-Borrower does not choose to have it considered as basis for repaying this loan.

		Monthly Amount
		$

IF EMPLOYED IN CURRENT POSITION FOR LESS THAN TWO YEARS COMPLETE THE FOLLOWING

B/C	Previous Employer/School	City/State	Type of Business	Position/Title	Dates From/To	Monthly Income

THESE QUESTIONS APPLY TO BOTH BORROWER AND CO-BORROWER

If a "yes" answer is given to a question in this column, please explain on an attached sheet.

	Borrower Yes or No	Co-Borrower Yes or No
Are there any outstanding judgements against you?	_____	_____
Have you been declared bankrupt within the past 7 years?	_____	_____
Have you had property disclosed upon or given title or deed in lieu thereof in the last 7 years?	_____	_____
Are you a party to a lawsuit?	_____	_____
Are you obliged to pay alimony, child support, or separate maintenance?	_____	_____
Is any part of the down payment borrowed?	_____	_____

	Borrower Yes or No	Co-Borrower Yes or No
Are you a co-maker or endorser on a note?	_____	_____
Are you a U.S. citizen?	_____	_____
If "no," are you a resident alien?	_____	_____
If "no," are you a non-resident alien?	_____	_____
Explain Other Financing or Other Equity (if any). _____		

* FHLMC/FNMA require business credit report, signed Federal Income Tax returns for the last two years, and, if available, audited Profit and Loss Statement plus balance sheet for same period.
** All present Monthly Housing Expenses of Borrower and Co-Borrower should be listed on a combined basis.
*** Optional for FHLMC.

STATEMENT OF ASSETS AND LIABILITIES

This Statement and any applicable supporting schedules may be completed jointly by both married and unmarried couples as owners if their assets and liabilities are sufficiently joined so that the Statement can be meaningfully and fairly represented on a combined basis; otherwise separate Statements and Schedules are required (FHLMC 65A/FNMA 1003A). If the co-borrower section was completed about a spouse, this statement and supporting schedules must be completed about that spouse also. ☐ Completed Jointly ☐ Not Completed Jointly

ASSETS		LIABILITIES AND PLEDGED ASSETS			
		Indicate by (*) those liabilities or pledged assets which will not be satisfied upon sale of real estate owned or upon refinancing of subject property.			
Description	Cash or Market Value	Creditor's Name, Address and Account Number	Acct. Name if Not Borrower's	Mo. Pmt. and Mos. Left to Pay	Unpaid Balance
Cash Deposit Toward Purchase Held By		**Installment Debts** (Include "revolving" charge accounts) Co. Address City	Acct. No.	$ Pmt./Mos.	$
Checking and Savings Accounts (Show Names of Institutions and Account Numbers) **Bank, S & L or Credit Union** Address City Acct. No.		Co. Address City	Acct. No.		
Bank, S & L or Credit Union Address City Acct. No.		Co. Address City	Acct. No.		
		Co. Address City	Acct. No.		
		Other Debts Including Stock Pledges			
Stocks and Bonds (No./Description)		**Real Estate Loans** Co. Address City	Acct. No.		
Life Insurance Net Cash Value Face Amount $		Co. Address City	Acct. No.		
Subtotal Liquid Assets		**Automobile Loans** Co. Address City	Acct. No.		
Real Estate Owned (Enter Market Value from Schedule of Real Estate Owned)					
Vested Interest in Retirement Fund		Co. Address City	Acct. No.		
Net Worth of Businesses Owned (ATTACH FINANCIAL STATEMENT)					
Automobile Owned (Make and Year)					
Furniture and Personal Property		**Alimony/Child Support/Separate Maintenance Payments Owed to**			
Other Assets (itemize)		**Total Monthly Payments**		$	
Total Assets	A $	**Net Worth (A minus B) $**		Total Liabilities	B $

SCHEDULE OF REAL ESTATE OWNED (if Additional Properties Owned Attach Separate Schedule)

Address of Property (indicate S if Sold, PS if Pending Sale, or R if Rental being held for income) ↓	Type of Property	Present Market Value	Amount of Mortgages & Liens	Gross Rental Income	Mortgage Payments	Taxes, Ins. Maintenance, Misc.	Net Rental Income
		$	$	$	$	$	$
TOTALS →		$	$	$	$	$	$

LIST PREVIOUS CREDIT REFERENCES

B=Borrower C=Co-Borrower	Creditor's Name and Address	Account Number	Purpose	Highest Balance	Date Paid
				$	

List any additional names under which credit has previously been received:

AGREEMENT: The undersigned applies for the loan indicated in this application to be secured by a first mortgage or deed of trust on the property described herein, and represents that the property will not be used for any illegal or restricted purpose, and that all statements made in this application are true and are made for the purpose of obtaining the loan. Verification may be obtained from any source named in this application. The original or a copy of this application will be retained by the lender, even if the loan is not granted. The undersigned ☐ intend or ☐ do not intend to occupy the property as their primary residence.

I/we fully understand that it is a federal crime punishable by fine or imprisonment, or both, to knowingly make any false statements concerning any of the above facts as applicable under the provisions of Title 18, United States Code, Section 1014.

_____ Date _____   _____ Date _____
Borrower's Signature   Co-Borrower's Signature

INFORMATION FOR GOVERNMENT MONITORING PURPOSES

The following information is requested by the Federal Government for certain types of loans related to a dwelling, in order to monitor the lender's compliance with equal credit opportunity and fair housing laws. You are not required to furnish this information, but are encouraged to do so. The law provides that a lender may neither discriminate on the basis of this information, nor on whether you choose to furnish it. However, if you choose not to furnish it, under Federal regulations this lender is required to note race and sex on the basis of visual observation and surname. If you do not wish to furnish the above information, please check the box below. (Lender must review the above material to assure that the disclosures satisfy all requirements to which the lender is subject under applicable state law for the particular type of loan applied for.

Borrower: ☐ I do not wish to furnish this information   Co-Borrower: ☐ I do not wish to furnish this information

Race/National Origin: Race/National Origin:

☐ American Indian, Alaskan Native   ☐ Asian, Pacific Islander   ☐ American Indian, Alaskan Native   ☐ Asian, Pacific Islander

☐ Black   ☐ Hispanic   ☐ White   ☐ Black   ☐ Hispanic   ☐ White

☐ Other (specify): _____   ☐ Other (specify): _____

Sex: ☐ Female   ☐ Male   Sex: ☐ Female   ☐ Male

TO BE COMPLETED BY INTERVIEWER

This application was taken by:
☐ face to face interview
☐ by mail
☐ by telephone

_____   _____
Interviewer   Name of Interviewer's Employer

_____   _____
Interviewer's Phone Number   Address of Interviewer's Employer

TRUTH-IN-LENDING DISCLOSURE STATEMENT

Borrower's Name (Last-First-Middle Initial) and Address (Street-City-State-Zip Code)	Date	Loan Number
	Lender Name	

TRUTH IN LENDING DISCLOSURE

ANNUAL PERCENTAGE RATE	FINANCE CHARGE	AMOUNT FINANCED	TOTAL OF PAYMENTS	*=ESTIMATED
The cost of your credit as a yearly rate	The dollar amount the credit will cost you	The amount of credit provided to you or on your behalf	The amount you will have paid when you have made all payments as scheduled	
%	$	$	$	

Payment Schedule	Total Payments	Filing/Recording Fees: $

Number of Payments	Amount of Payments (Principal & Interest & Private Mortgage Insurance, if applicable)	When Payments are Due

ADJUSTABLE RATE FEATURE:

_____ This loan does not have an adjustable rate feature.

_____ This loan has an adjustable rate feature. Disclosures about the adjustable rate feature have been provided to you earlier.

SECURITY: You are giving a security interest in the property located at:

LATE CHARGES: If your payment is more than _____ days delinquent, a late charge of ____% of the monthly principal and interest payment will be assessed.

ASSUMPTION: Someone buying your home

_____ Cannot assume the remainder of the mortgage on the original terms

_____ May, subject to conditions, be allowed to assume the remainder of the mortgage on the original terms.

PREPAYMENT: If you payoff early, you

_____ may _____ will not   have to pay a penalty

_____ may _____ will not   be entitled to a refund of part of the refinance charge.

See your contract documents for any additional information regarding non-payment, default, required re-payment in full before scheduled date and payment refunds and penalties.

INSURANCE: Hazard insurance in the amount of $_____ and flood insurance in the amount of $_____ with loss payable clause to the lender required as a condition of this loan. This insurance may be purchased from any insurance company of the Borrower's choice who is acceptable to the Lender.

Credit life or disability insurance is not required in connection with this transaction. If such coverage is desired, it may be purchased through any person of Borrower's choice or it is available through Lender upon submission of a separate application. This insurance is not in effect and no charge is made for such coverage until a separate application has been submitted and approved.

ITEMIZATION OF THE AMOUNT FINANCED

Loan Amount	Prepaid Finance Charge	Note Interest Rate	Loan Type
$	$		

I/We hereby acknowledge reading and receiving a complete copy of this disclosure along with copies of documents referred to in this disclosure.

_____ _____ _____ _____
Borrower/Signature   Date   Co-Borrower/Signature   Date

RESIDENTIAL REAL ESTATE SALES DISCLOSURE

THE PROSPECTIVE BUYER AND THE OWNER MAY WISH TO OBTAIN PROFESSIONAL ADVICE OR INSPECTIONS OF THE PROPERTY AND PROVIDE FOR APPROPRIATE PROVISIONS IN A CONTRACT BETWEEN THEM CONCERNING ANY ADVICE, INSPECTIONS, DEFECTS, OR WARRANTIES OBTAINED ON THE PROPERTY. THE REPRESENTATIONS IN THIS FORM ARE REPRESENTATIONS OF THE OWNER AND ARE NOT REPRESENTATIONS OF THE AGENT, IF ANY. THIS INFORMATION IS FOR DISCLOSURE ONLY AND IS NOT INTENDED TO BE A PART OF THE CONTRACT BETWEEN THE BUYER AND OWNER.

Seller states that the information contained in this Disclosure is correct as of the date below,
to the best of the Seller's current actual knowledge.

DATE _____ PROPERTY ADDRESS _____

THE CONDITION OF THE FOLLOWING PROPERTY IS:	N/A	DEFECTIVE	NOT DEFECTIVE	UNKNOWN
1. ELECTRICAL SYSTEM				
a) Air filtration system				
b) Burglar alarm				
c) Cable TV wiring and connections				
d) Ceiling fans				
e) Garage door opener				
f) Inside telephone wiring and jacks				
g) Intercom				
h) Kitchen range hood				
i) Light fixtures				
j) Sauna				
k) Smoke/fire alarm				
l) Switches and outlets				
m) Amp services				
n) Other				
2. HEATING AND COOLING				
a) Attic fan				
b) Central air conditioning				
c) Hot water heater				
d) Furnace heater-gas, electric, oil, solar				
e) Fireplace				
f) Humidifier				
g) Propane tank				
h) Other				
3. APPLIANCES				
a) Vacuum system (built-in)				
b) Clothes washing machine				
c) Clothes dryer				
d) Compactor				
e) Convection oven				
f) Dishwasher				
g) Freezer				
h) Garbage disposal				
i) Gas grill				
j) Microwave oven				
k) Oven				
l) Range				
m) Refrigerator				
n) TV antenna/dish				
o) Other				

	N/A	DEFECTIVE	NOT DEFECTIVE	UNKNOWN
4. WATER & SEWER SYSTEM				
a) Cistern				
b) Septic field/bed				
c) Hot tub				
d) Plumbing				
e) Aerator system				
f) Sump pump				
g) Sprinkler /irrigation system				
h) Water heater-gas, electric, solar				
i) Water filtration system				
j) Water softener				
k) Well				
l) Public water system				
m) Public sewer system				
n) Private/community water system				
o) Private/community sewer system				
p) Other systems				

	YES	NO	UNKNOWN
5. FOUNDATION & STRUCTURE			
a) Are there any problems with the foundation?			
b) Are there any structural problems with the building?			
c) Have any substantial additions or alterations been made without a required building permit?			
d) Are there any violations of zoning, building codes or restrictive covenants?			
e) Are there moisture or water problems?			
f) Is there termite, rodent or insect damage?			
g) Is there damage due to wind or flood?			
h) Is the property in a flood plain?			
i) Is the proeprty located within 1 (one) nautical mile of an airport?			
j) Is there any threat of or pending litigation regarding the property?			
k) Are the furnace, wood stove, chimney/flue in working order?			
6. ROOF			
a) Age in years_____			
b) Are there any current leaks?			
c) Is roof currently damaged?			
d) Is there more than one roof on the structure? If yes, how many_____?			

7. HAZARDOUS CONDITIONS

Are there any existing hazards on the property such as methane gas, radioactive material, radon or lead paint in house or well, or expansive soil, toxic materials, asbestos insulation, landfill, mineshaft or PCBs? If yes, explain:

8. Additional comments or explanations:

Seller and Buyer hereby acknowledge receipt of this Disclosure Form by signing below:

Seller's Signature	Date	Buyer's Signature	Date
Seller's Name		Buyer's Name	
Seller's Signature	Date	Buyer's Signature	Date
Seller's Name		Buyer's Name	

SCHEDULE OF PROGRESS - BUYER

TASK	TARGET DATE	COMPLETION DATE
Review Ads	_____	_____
Visit Homes	_____	_____
Make an Offer	_____	_____
Sign Disclosure	_____	_____
Sign Contract	_____	_____
Deposit earnest money	_____	_____
Get home inspected	_____	_____
Resolve contingencies	_____	_____
Apply for loan	_____	_____
Loan sent to underwriting	_____	_____
Receive loan approval	_____	_____
Send commitment letter	_____	_____
Complete title work	_____	_____
Get home appraised	_____	_____
Receive appraisal results	_____	_____
Obtain hazard insurance	_____	_____
Settlement - closing statement	_____	_____

SCHEDULE OF PROGRESS - SELLER

TASK	TARGET DATE	COMPLETION DATE
Place Ad	_____	_____
Open House	_____	_____
Review Offers	_____	_____
Submit Disclosure	_____	_____
Sign Contract	_____	_____
Deposit earnest money	_____	_____
Buyer's Inspection	_____	_____
Resolve contingencies	_____	_____
Buyer applies for loan	_____	_____
Buyer loan approved	_____	_____
Receive commitment letter	_____	_____
Complete title work	_____	_____
Appraisal date	_____	_____
Receive appraisal results	_____	_____
Settlement - closing statement	_____	_____

A. **Settlement Statement**

B. Type of Loan

	6. File Number	7. Loan Number	8. Mortgage Insurance Case Number

C. NOTE: This form is furnished to give you a statement of actual settlement costs. Amounts paid to and by the settlement agent are shown. Items marked "(p.o.c.)" were paid outside the closing; they are shown here for informational purposes and are not included in the totals.

D. Name and Address of Borrower	E. Name and Address of Seller	F. Name and Address of Lender
		H. Settlement Agent
G. Property Location	Place of Settlement	
	I. SETTLEMENT DATE:	

J. SUMMARY OF BORROWER'S TRANSACTION			
100. GROSS AMOUNT DUE FROM BORROWER		207.	
101. Contract sales price		208.	
102. Personal property		209.	
103. Settlement charges to borrower (line 1400)		209a	
104.		209b	
105.		Adjustments for items upaid by seller	
Adjustments for items paid by seller in advance		210. City/town taxes to	
106. City/town taxes to		211. County taxes to	
107. County taxes to		212. Assessments to	
108. Assessments to		213.	
109.		214.	
110.		215.	
111.		216.	
112.		217.	
120. GROSS AMOUNT DUE FROM BORROWER		218.	
		219.	
200. AMOUNTS PAID BY OR IN BEHALF OF BORROWER		220. TOTAL AMOUNTS PAID BY OR IN BEHALF OF BORROWER	
201. Deposit or earnest money		**300. CASH AT SETTLEMENT FROM/TO BORROWER**	
202. Principal amount of new loan(s)		301. Gross amount due from borrower (line 120)	
203. Existing loan(s) taken subject to		302. Less amounts paid by/for borrower (line 220)	( )
204.		303. CASH ❏ From ❏ To **BORROWER**	
205.			
206.			

PAGE 1

127

K. SUMMARY OF SELLER'S TRANSACTION

400. GROSS AMOUNT DUE TO SELLER		507.	
401. Contract sales price		508.	
402. Personal property		509.	
403.		509a	
404.		509b	
405.		*Adjustments for items upaid by seller*	
Adjustments for items paid by seller in advance		510. City/town taxes to	
406. City/town taxes to		511. County taxes to	
407. County taxes to		512. Assessments to	
408. Assessments to		513.	
409.		514.	
410.		515.	
411.		516.	
412.		517.	
420. GROSS AMOUNT DUE TO SELLER		518.	
500. REDUCTIONS IN AMOUNT DUE TO SELLER		519.	
		520. TOTAL REDUCTIONS IN AMOUNT DUE SELLER	
501. Excess deposit (see instructions)		**600. CASH AT SETTLEMENT TO/FROM SELLER**	
502. Settlement charges to seller (line 1400)		601. Gross amount due to seller (line 420)	
503. Existing loan(s) taken subject to		602. Less reductions in amount due seller (line 520)	( )
504. Payoff of first mortgage loan			
505.		603. CASH ❑ To ❑ From **SELLER**	
506. Payoff of second mortgage loan			

L. Settlement Charges		Paid From Borrower's Funds At Settlement	Paid From Seller's Funds At Settlement
700. TOTAL SALES/BROKER'S COM. based on price $ @ % =			
Division of Commission (line 700) as follows:			
701. $ to			
702. $ to			
703. Commission paid at Settlement			
704.			
800. Items Payable In Connection With Loan			
801. Loan Origination Fee %			
802. Loan Discount %			
803. Appraisal Fee to			
804. Credit Report to			
805. Lender's Inspection Fee			
806.			
807.			
808.			
809.			
810.			
811.			
900. Items Required By Lender To Be Paid In Advance			
901. Interest from to @ $ /day			
902. Mortgage Insurance Premium for months to			
903. Hazard Insurance Premium for years to			
904.			
905.			

PAGE 2

1000.	**Reserves Deposited With Lender**				
1001.	Hazard Insurance	months@ $	per month		
1002.	Mortgage Insurance	months@ $	per month		
1003.	City Property Taxes	months@ $	per month		
1004.	County Property Taxes	months@ $	per month		
1005.	Annual Assessments	months@ $	per month		
1006.		months@ $	per month		
1007.		months@ $	per month		
1008.		months@ $	per month		
1100.	**Title Charges**				
1101.	Settlement or closing fee	to			
1102.	Abstract or title search	to			
1103.	Title examination	to			
1104.	Title insurance binder	to			
1105.	Document preparation	to			
1106.	Notary fees	to			
1107.	Attorney's fees				
	(includes above items numbers:)				
1108.	Title insurance: Risk Premium				
	(includes above items numbers:)				
1109.	Lender's coverage: Risk Premium $				
1110.	Owner's coverage: Risk Premium $				
1110a	Endorsements:				
1111.					
1112.					
1113.					
1200.	**Government Recording and Transfer Charges**				
1201.	Recording fees: Deed $	Mortgage(s) $	Releases $		
1202.	City/county tax/stamps: Deed $	Mortgage(s) $			
1203.	State tax/stamps: Deed $	Mortgage(s) $			
1204.					
1205.					
1300.	**Additional Settlement Charges**				
1301.	Survey	to			
1302.	Pest inspection	to			
1303.					
1304.					
1305.					
1306.					
1307.					
1400.	**Total Settlement Charges** (enter on lines 103, Section J and 502, Section K)				

CERTIFICATION

I have carefully reviewed the Settlement Statement and to the best of my knowledge and belief, it is a true and accurate statement of all receipts and disbursements made on my account or by me in this transaction. I further certify that I have received a copy of the Settlement Statement.

_____ Borrower   _____ Seller

_____ Borrower   _____ Seller

The Settlement Statement which I have prepared is a true and accurate account of this transaction. I have caused, or will cause, the funds to be disbursed in accordance with this statement.

_____ Settlement Agent   _____ Date

WARNING: It is a crime to knowingly make false statements to the United States on this or any other similar form. Penalties upon conviction can include a fine and imprisonmen t. For details see: Title 18 U.S. Code Section 1001 and Section 1010.

WARRANTY DEED

For good consideration, we

of   , County of   , State of
                , hereby bargain, deed and convey to   of
                                            , County of   , State of
                , the following described land in   County, free
and clear with WARRANTY COVENANTS; to wit:

Grantor(s), for itself and its heirs, hereby covenants with Grantee, its heirs, and assigns, that Grantor(s) is lawfully seized in fee simple of the above-described premises; that it has a good right to convey; that the premises are free from all encumbrances; that Grantor(s) and its heirs, and all persons acquiring any interest in the property granted, through or for Grantor(s), will, on demand of Grantee, or its heirs or assigns, and at the expense of Grantee, its heirs or assigns, execute any instrument necessary for the further assurance of the title to the premises that may be reasonably required; and that Grantor(s) and its heirs will forever warrant and defend all of the property so granted to Grantee, its heirs, and assigns, against every person lawfully claiming the same or any part thereof.

Being the same property conveyed to the Grantor(s) by deed of   , dated
        , 19   .

WITNESS the hands and seal of said Grantor(s) this   day of   , 19   .

_____
Grantor

_____
Grantor

STATE OF   }
COUNTY OF   }

On   before me,   , personally appeared
                                          , personally known to me (or
proved to me on the basis of satisfactory evidence) to be the person(s) whose name(s) is/are subscribed to the within instrument and acknowledged to me that he/she/they executed the same in
his/her/their authorized capacity(ies), and that by his/her/their signature(s) on the instrument the
person(s), or the entity upon behalf of which the person(s) acted, executed the instrument.
WITNESS my hand and official seal.

Signature_____   Affiant ____Known ____Unknown
                                         ID Produced_____
                                                              (Seal)

_____
Signature of Preparer

_____
Print name of Preparer

_____
Address of Preparer

_____
City, State, Zip

Buying / Selling Your Home

How To Save On Attorney Fees

Millions of Americans know they need legal protection, whether it's to get agreements in writing, protect themselves from lawsuits, or document business transactions. But too often these basic but important legal matters are neglected because of something else millions of Americans know: legal services are expensive.

They don't have to be. In response to the demand for affordable legal protection and services, there are now specialized clinics that process simple documents. Paralegals help people prepare legal claims on a freelance basis. People find they can handle their own legal affairs with do-it-yourself legal guides and kits. Indeed, this book is a part of this growing trend.

When are these alternatives to a lawyer appropriate? If you hire an attorney, how can you make sure you're getting good advice for a reasonable fee? Most importantly, do you know how to lower your legal expenses?

When there is no alternative

Make no mistake: serious legal matters require a lawyer. The tips in this book can help you reduce your legal fees, but there is no alternative to good professional legal services in certain circumstances:

- when you are charged with a felony, you are a repeat offender, or jail is possible
- when a substantial amount of money or property is at stake in a lawsuit
- when you are a party in an adversarial divorce or custody case
- when you are an alien facing deportation

- when you are the plaintiff in a personal injury suit that involves large sums of money
- when you're involved in very important transactions

Are you sure you want to take it to court?

Consider the following questions before you pursue legal action:

 What are your financial resources?

Money buys experienced attorneys, and experience wins over first-year lawyers and public defenders. Even with a strong case, you may save money by not going to court. Yes, people win millions in court. But for every big winner there are ten plaintiffs who either lose or win so little that litigation wasn't worth their effort.

 Do you have the time and energy for a trial?

Courts are overbooked, and by the time your case is heard your initial zeal may have grown cold. If you can, make a reasonable settlement out of court. On personal matters, like a divorce or custody case, consider the emotional toll on all parties. Any legal case will affect you in some way. You will need time away from work. A newsworthy case may bring press coverage. Your loved ones, too, may face publicity. There is usually good reason to settle most cases quickly, quietly, and economically.

 How can you settle your disputes without litigation?

Consider *mediation.* In mediation, each party pays half the mediator's fee and, together, they attempt to work out a compromise informally. *Binding arbitration* is another alternative. For a small fee, a trained specialist serves as judge, hears both sides, and hands down a ruling that both parties have agreed to accept.

So you need an attorney

Having done your best to avoid litigation, if you still find yourself headed for court, you will need an attorney. To get the right attorney at a reasonable cost, be guided by these four questions:

 What type of case is it?

You don't seek a foot doctor for a toothache. Find an attorney experienced in your type of legal problem. If you can get recommendations from clients who have recently won similar cases, do so.

Where will the trial be held?

You want a lawyer familiar with that court system and one who knows the court personnel and the local protocol—which can vary from one locality to another.

 Should you hire a large or small firm?

Hiring a senior partner at a large and prestigious law firm sounds reassuring, but chances are the actual work will be handled by associates – at high rates. Small firms may give your case more attention but, with fewer resources, take longer to get the work done.

 What can you afford?

Hire an attorney you can afford, of course, but know what a fee quote includes. High fees may reflect a firm's luxurious offices, high-paid staff and unmonitored expenses, while low estimates may mean "unexpected" costs later. Ask for a written estimate of all costs and anticipated expenses.

How to find a good lawyer ▬▬▬▬▬▬

Whether you need an attorney quickly or you're simply open to future possibilities, here are seven nontraditional methods for finding your lawyer:

1) *Word of mouth:* Successful lawyers develop reputations. Your friends, business associates and other professionals are potential referral sources. But beware of hiring a friend. Keep the client-attorney relationship strictly business.

2) *Directories:* The Yellow Pages and the Martin-Hubbell Lawyer Directory (in your local library) can help you locate a lawyer with the right education, background and expertise for your case.

3) *Databases:* A paralegal should be able to run a quick computer search of local attorneys for you using the Westlaw or Lexis database.

4) *State bar association:* Bar associations are listed in phone books. Along with lawyer referrals, your bar association can direct you to low-cost legal clinics or specialists in your area.

5) *Law schools:* Did you know that a legal clinic run by a law school gives law students hands-on experience? This may fit your legal needs. A third-year law student loaded with enthusiasm and a little experience might fill the bill quite inexpensively—or even for free.

6) *Advertisements:* Ads are a lawyer's business card. If a "TV attorney" seems to have a good track record with your kind of

---

Highlight

High fees may reflect a firm's luxurious offices, high-paid staff and unmonitored expenses, while low estimates may mean "unexpected" costs later.

---

case, why not call? Just don't be swayed by the glamour of a high-profile attorney.

7) *Your own ad:* A small ad describing the qualifications and legal expertise you're seeking, placed in a local bar association journal, may get you just the lead you need.

How to hire and work with your attorney

No matter how you hear about an attorney, you must interview him or her in person. Call the office during business hours and ask to speak to the attorney directly. Then explain your case briefly and mention how you obtained the attorney's name. If the attorney sounds interested and knowledgeable, arrange for a visit.

The ten-point visit:

1) Note the address. This is a good indication of the rates to expect.

2) Note the condition of the offices. File-laden desks and poorly maintained work space may indicate a poorly run firm.

3) Look for up-to-date computer equipment and an adequate complement of support personnel.

4) Note the appearance of the attorney. How will he or she impress a judge or jury?

5) Is the attorney attentive? Does the attorney take notes, ask questions, follow up on points you've mentioned?

6) Ask what schools he or she has graduated from, and feel free to check credentials with the state bar association.

7) Does the attorney have a good track record with your type of case?

8) Does he or she explain legal terms to you in plain English?

9) Are the firm's costs reasonable?

10) Will the attorney provide references?

Hiring the attorney

Having chosen your attorney, make sure all the terms are agreeable. Send letters to any other attorneys you have interviewed, thanking them for their time and interest in your case and explaining that you have retained another attorney's services.

Highlight

Explain your case briefly and mention how you obtained the attorney's name. If the attorney sounds interested and knowledgeable, arrange for a visit.

Request a letter from your new attorney outlining your retainer agreement. The letter should list all fees you will be responsible for as well as the billing arrangement. Did you arrange to pay in installments? This should be noted in your retainer agreement.

Controlling legal costs

Legal fees and expenses can get out of control easily, but the client who is willing to put in the effort can keep legal costs manageable. Work out a budget with your attorney. Create a timeline for your case. Estimate the costs involved in each step.

Legal fees can be straightforward. Some lawyers charge a fixed rate for a specific project. Others charge contingency fees (they collect a percentage of your recovery, usually 35-50 percent, if you win and nothing if you lose). But most attorneys prefer to bill by the hour. Expenses can run the gamut, with one hourly charge for taking depositions and another for making copies.

Have your attorney give you a list of charges for services rendered and an itemized monthly bill. The bill should explain the service performed, who performed the work, when the service was provided, how long it took, and how the service benefits your case.

Ample opportunity abounds in legal billing for dishonesty and greed. There is also plenty of opportunity for knowledgeable clients to cut their bills significantly if they know what to look for. Asking the right questions and setting limits on fees is smart and can save you a bundle. Don't be afraid to question legal bills. It's your case and your money!

When the bill arrives

- *Retainer fees:* You should already have a written retainer agreement. Ideally, the retainer fee applies toward case costs, and your agreement puts that in writing. Protect yourself by escrowing the retainer fee until the case has been handled to your satisfaction.

- *Office visit charges:* Track your case and all documents, correspondence, and bills. Diary all dates, deadlines and questions you want to ask your attorney during your next office visit. This keeps expensive office visits focused and productive, with more accomplished in less time. If your attorney charges less for phone consultations than office visits, reserve visits for those tasks that must be done in person.

- *Phone bills:* This is where itemized bills are essential. Who made the call, who was spoken to, what was discussed, when was the call made, and how long did it last? Question any charges that seem unnecessary or excessive (over 60 minutes).

- *Administrative costs:* Your case may involve hundreds, if not thousands, of documents: motions, affidavits, depositions, interrogatories, bills, memoranda, and letters. Are they all necessary? Understand your attorney's case strategy before paying for an endless stream of costly documents.

- *Associate and paralegal fees:* Note in your retainer agreement which staff people will have access to your file. Then you'll have an informed and efficient staff working on your case, and you'll recognize their names on your bill. Of course, your attorney should handle the important part of your case, but less costly paralegals or associates may handle routine matters more economically. Note: Some firms expect their associates to meet a quota of billable hours, although the time spent is not always warranted. Review your bill. Does the time spent make sense for the document in question? Are several staff involved in matters that should be handled by one person? Don't be afraid to ask questions. And withhold payment until you have satisfactory answers.

- *Court stenographer fees:* Depositions and court hearings require costly transcripts and stenographers. This means added expenses. Keep an eye on these costs.

- *Copying charges:* Your retainer fee should limit the number of copies made of your complete file. This is in your legal interest, because multiple files mean multiple chances others may access your confidential information. It is also in your financial interest, because copying costs can be astronomical.

- *Fax costs:* As with the phone and copier, the fax can easily run up costs. Set a limit.

- *Postage charges:* Be aware of how much it costs to send a legal document overnight, or a registered letter. Offer to pick up or deliver expensive items when it makes sense.

- *Filing fees:* Make it clear to your attorney that you want to minimize the number of court filings in your case. Watch your bill and question any filing that seems unnecessary.

- *Document production fee:* Turning over documents to your opponent is mandatory and expensive. If you're faced with

Highlight

Note in your retainer agreement which staff people will have access to your file. Then you'll have an informed and efficient staff working on your case, and you'll recognize their names on your bill.

Highlight

Surprise costs are so
routine they're predictable.
Budget a few thousand
dollars over what you
estimate your case will
cost. It usually is needed.

reproducing boxes of documents, consider having the job done by a commercial firm rather than your attorney's office.

- *Research and investigations:* Pay only for photographs that can be used in court. Can you hire a photographer at a lower rate than what your attorney charges? Reserve that right in your retainer agreement. Database research can also be extensive and expensive; if your attorney uses Westlaw or Nexis, set limits on the research you will pay for.

- *Expert witnesses:* Question your attorney if you are expected to pay for more than a reasonable number of expert witnesses. Limit the number to what is essential to your case.

- *Technology costs:* Avoid videos, tape recordings, and graphics if you can use old-fashioned diagrams to illustrate your case.

- *Travel expenses:* Travel expenses for those connected to your case can be quite costly unless you set a maximum budget. Check all travel-related items on your bill, and make sure they are appropriate. Always question why the travel is necessary before you agree to pay for it.

- *Appeals costs:* Losing a case often means an appeal, but weigh the costs involved before you make that decision. If money is at stake, do a cost-benefit analysis to see if an appeal is financially justified.

- *Monetary damages:* Your attorney should be able to help you estimate the total damages you will have to pay if you lose a civil case. Always consider settling out of court rather than proceeding to trial when the trial costs will be high.

- *Surprise costs:* Surprise costs are so routine they're predictable. The judge may impose unexpected court orders on one or both sides, or the opposition will file an unexpected motion that increases your legal costs. Budget a few thousand dollars over what you estimate your case will cost. It usually is needed.

- *Padded expenses:* Assume your costs and expenses are legitimate. But some firms do inflate expenses—office supplies, database searches, copying, postage, phone bills—to bolster their bottom line. Request copies of bills your law firm receives from support services. If you are not the only client represented on a bill, determine those charges related to your case.

Keeping it legal without a lawyer ■■■■

The best way to save legal costs is to avoid legal problems. There are hundreds of ways to decrease your chances of lawsuits and other nasty legal encounters. Most simply involve a little common sense. You can also use your own initiative to find and use the variety of self-help legal aid available to consumers.

11 situations in which you may not need a lawyer ■■■■

1) *No-fault divorce:* Married couples with no children, minimal property, and no demands for alimony can take advantage of divorce mediation services. A lawyer should review your divorce agreement before you sign it, but you will have saved a fortune in attorney fees. A marital or family counselor may save a seemingly doomed marriage, or help both parties move beyond anger to a calm settlement. Either way, counseling can save you money.

2) *Wills:* Do-it-yourself wills and living trusts are ideal for people with estates of less than $600,000. Even if an attorney reviews your final documents, a will kit allows you to read the documents, ponder your bequests, fill out sample forms, and discuss your wishes with your family at your leisure, without a lawyer's meter running.

3) *Incorporating:* Incorporating a small business can be done by any business owner. Your state government office provides the forms and instructions necessary. A visit to your state offices will probably be necessary to perform a business name check. A fee of $100-$200 is usually charged for processing your Articles of Incorporation. The rest is paperwork: filling out forms correctly; holding regular, official meetings; and maintaining accurate records.

4) *Routine business transactions:* Copyrights, for example, can be applied for by asking the U.S. Copyright Office for the appropriate forms and brochures. The same is true of the U.S. Patent and Trademark Office. If your business does a great deal of document preparation and research, hire a certified paralegal rather than paying an attorney's rates. Consider mediation or binding arbitration rather than going to court for a business dispute. Hire a human resources/benefits administrator to head off disputes concerning discrimination or other employee charges.

Highlight

The best way to save legal costs is to avoid legal problems.

5) *Repairing bad credit:* When money matters get out of hand, attorneys and bankruptcy should not be your first solution. Contact a credit counseling organization that will help you work out manageable payment plans so that everyone wins. It can also help you learn to manage your money better. A good company to start with is the Consumer Credit Counseling Service, 1-800-388-2227.

6) *Small Claims Court:* For legal grievances amounting to a few thousand dollars in damages, represent yourself in Small Claims Court. There is a small filing fee, forms to fill out, and several court visits necessary. If you can collect evidence, state your case in a clear and logical presentation, and come across as neat, respectful and sincere, you can succeed in Small Claims Court.

7) *Traffic Court:* Like Small Claims Court, Traffic Court may show more compassion to a defendant appearing without an attorney. If you are ticketed for a minor offense and want to take it to court, you will be asked to plead guilty or not guilty. If you plead guilty, you can ask for leniency in sentencing by presenting mitigating circumstances. Bring any witnesses who can support your story, and remember that presentation (some would call it acting ability) is as important as fact.

8) *Residential zoning petition:* If a homeowner wants to open a home business, build an addition, or make other changes that may affect his or her neighborhood, town approval is required. But you don't need a lawyer to fill out a zoning variance application, turn it in, and present your story at a public hearing. Getting local support before the hearing is the best way to assure a positive vote; contact as many neighbors as possible to reassure them that your plans won't adversely affect them or the neighborhood.

9) *Government benefit applications:* Applying for veterans' or unemployment benefits may be daunting, but the process doesn't require legal help. Apply for either immediately upon becoming eligible. Note: If your former employer contests your application for unemployment benefits and you have to defend yourself at a hearing, you may want to consider hiring an attorney.

10) *Receiving government files:* The Freedom of Information Act gives every American the right to receive copies of government information about him or her. Write a letter to the appropriate state or federal agency, noting the precise information you want. List each document

---

Highlight

If your business does a great deal of document preparation and research, hire a certified paralegal rather than paying an attorney's rates.

---

in a separate paragraph. Mention the Freedom of Information Act, and state that you will pay any expenses. Close with your signature and the address the documents should be sent to. An approved request may take six months to arrive. If it is refused on the grounds that the information is classified or violates another's privacy, send a letter of appeal explaining why the released information would not endanger anyone. Enlist the support of your local state or federal representative, if possible, to smooth the approval process.

11) *Citizenship:* Arriving in the United States to work and become a citizen is a process tangled in bureaucratic red tape, but it requires more perseverance than legal assistance. Immigrants can learn how to obtain a "Green Card," under what circumstances they can work, and what the requirements of citizenship are by contacting the Immigration Services or reading a good self-help book.

Save more; it's E-Z

When it comes to saving attorneys' fees, E-Z Legal Forms is the consumer's best friend. America's largest publisher of self-help legal products offers legally valid forms for virtually every situation. E-Z Legal Kits and E-Z Legal Guides include all necessary forms with a simple-to-follow manual of instructions or a layman's book. E-Z Legal Books are a legal library of forms and documents for everyday business and personal needs. E-Z Legal Software provides those same forms on disk and CD for customized documents at the touch of the keyboard.

You can add to your legal savvy and your ability to protect yourself, your loved ones, your business and your property with a range of self-help legal titles available through E-Z Legal Forms. See the product descriptions and information at the back of this guide.

Highlight

Arriving in the United States to work and become a citizen is a process tangled in bureaucratic red tape, but it requires more perseverance than legal assistance.

(How To Save On Attorney Fees was compiled and written by Valerie Hope Goldstein.)

Turn your computer into your own personal lawyer with *E·Z Legal*® *Software.*

The E-Z Way to Save TIME and MONEY! Customize, file and print professional forms from your computer! Only $29⁹⁵*!

Our Windows programs are as E-Z as 1-2-3!

1) Customize, save and print in minutes! Loads quickly from 3.5" Disk or CD, both included in the package.

2) Just click on a form to open it. E-Z category menu and dialog box help you find the form you need.

3) Fill in the form with the help of simple step-by-step instructions.

Three new programs for 1997!

E-Z Construction Estimator   Item No. CD316

Every contractor can profit from this time-saving software. It automatically calculates the detailed costs of a given project, from equipment to labor.

Buying/Selling Your Home   Item No. SW1111

Save thousands of dollars in broker's fees by buying or selling your home yourself.

W-2 MAKER   Available September 1997!

A must for every business! Completing end-of-the-year tax forms for your employees is just a click away!

☑ *Check out the*
E•Z LEGAL® LIBRARY

Valid in all 50 states

☑ GUIDES

Each comprehensive guide contains the valid forms, samples, instructions, information and suggestions you need to proceed.

Plus state-by-state requirements (where appropriate), a handy glossary and the valuable 10-page supplement "How to Save on Attorney Fees."

☑ KITS

Each kit includes a clear, concise instruction manual to help you understand your rights and obligations, plus the ready-to-complete forms you need.

For the busy do-it-yourselfer, it's quick, it's affordable, it's E-Z.

TITLES

✔ **Bankruptcy**
Take the confusion out of filing bankruptcy.

✔ **Buying/Selling a Home****
Learn the ins and outs of moving in or out.

✔ **Collecting Child Support****
Ensure your kids the support they deserve.

✔ **Credit Repair**
It's got all the tools to put you back on track.

✔ **Divorce**
Learn to proceed on your own, without a lawyer.

✔ **Employment Law***
A handy reference for employers and employees.

✔ **Immigration***
A must-have for immigrants and aliens.

✔ **Incorporation**
Information you need to get your company Inc'ed.

✔ **Last Will & Testament**
Write a will the right way, the E-Z way.

✔ **Limited Liability Company****
Learn all about the hottest new business entity.

✔ **Living Will & P.O.A. for Healthcare**
Take steps now to ensure Death with Dignity.

✔ **Living Trust**
Trust us to help you provide for your loved ones.

✔ **Small Claims Court**
Prepare for court... or explore other avenues.

✔ **Trademarks & Copyrights***
Forms to obtain your own copyright or trademark.

✔ **Traffic Court**
Learn your rights on the road and in court.

*available as guide only   **available as kit only

LEGAL LIBRARY CARD

E•Z LEGAL FORMS®

... when you need it in writing!®

Valid at:
Super Stores, Office Supply Stores,
Drug Stores, Hardware Stores, Bookstores
and other fine retailers.

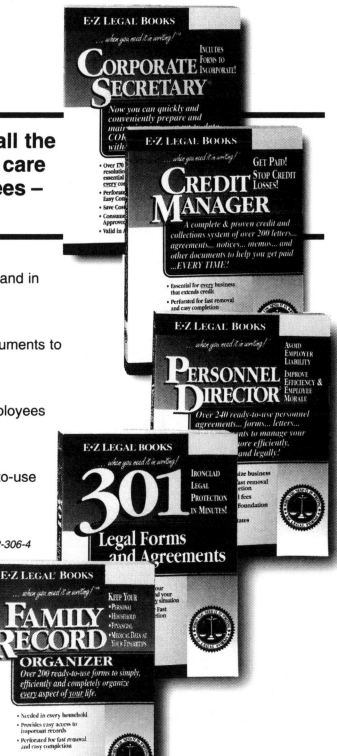

	Item#	Qty.	Price Ea.
★ **E•Z Legal Kits**			
Bankruptcy	K100		$21.95
Incorporation	K101		$21.95
Divorce	K102		$27.95
Credit Repair	K103		$18.95
Living Trust	K105		$18.95
Living Will	K106		$21.95
Last Will & Testament	K107		$16.95
Small Claims Court	K109		$19.95
Traffic Court	K110		$19.95
Buying/Selling Your Home	K111		$18.95
Collecting Child Support	K115		$18.95
Limited Liability Company	K116		$18.95
★ **E•Z Legal Software**			
Business Lawyer	CD311		$29.95
Personnel Director	CD312		$29.95
Corporate Secretary	CD314		$29.95
E-Z Construction Estimator	CD316		$29.95
Credit Repair	SW1103		$29.95
Incorporation	SW1101		$29.95
Divorce	SW1102		$29.95
Living Trust	SW1105		$29.95
Last Will & Testament	SW1107		$14.95
Buying/Selling Your Home	SW1111		$29.95
Family Record Organizer	SW306		$14.95
★ **E•Z Legal Books**			
Family Record Organizer	BK300		$24.95
301 Legal Forms & Agreements	BK301		$24.95
Personnel Director	BK302		$24.95
Credit Manager	BK303		$24.95
Corporate Secretary	BK304		$24.95
E-Z Legal Advisor	LA101		$24.95
★ **E•Z Legal Guides**			
Bankruptcy	G100		$14.95
Incorporation	G101		$14.95
Divorce	G102		$14.95
Credit Repair	G103		$14.95
Living Trust	G105		$14.95
Living Will/P.O.A. for Health Care	G106		$14.95
Last Will & Testament	G107		$14.95
Small Claims Court	G109		$14.95
Traffic Court	G110		$14.95
Employment Law	G112		$14.95
Immigration (English only)	G113		$14.95
Trademarks & Copyrights	G114		$14.95
★ **Labor Law Posters**			
Federal Labor Law Poster	LP001		$11.99
State Labor Law Poster (specify state)			$29.95
★ TOTAL # OF ITEMS			
★ SHIPPING & HANDLING*			$
★ **TOTAL OF ORDER****:			$

ss E-Z ord.2-97

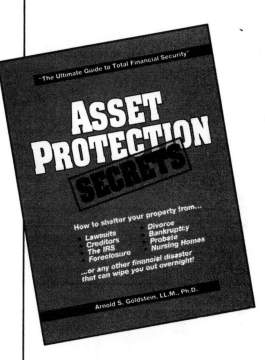

Index